The Snatch Back:

Reclaiming Your Life One Truth at a Time

by

Monique Carkum Edwards

D1602923

The Snatch Back: Reclaiming Your Life One Truth at a Time

Copyright 2020 by Monique Carkum Edwards

All rights reserved, Printed in the United States of America. No part of this book may be used or reproduced in any manner whatsoever without written permission except in the case of brief quotations embodied in critical articles or reviews.

For information contact

http://moniquecarkumedwards.com

First Edition: September 2020

Introduction

"Get her to the ER *immediately*! We need to rule out the possibility of a stroke." I could hear my doctor through the cell phone my husband Lennon was holding as he bent over me. Though typically cool as a cucumber under pressure, I could see the growing concern on his face. Our children, Brooklynn and Judah, surrounded me, holding my hands and trying not to look terrified. Lennon prayed over me while simultaneously calculating in his head whether to call an ambulance or try to get me up and to our car so he could drive me to the emergency room himself. Just moments earlier, I had collapsed in the foyer of our home. As I lay there with no feeling in some of my extremities and pain in others, my speech slurred and unable to gather my thoughts to form complete sentences, I wondered "*How in the world did I end up here?*"

Maybe you're a millennial staring at a mountain of student loan debt for an education that was supposed to lead to a dream career, but your current job is a nightmare. Perhaps you're forty-ish with a couple of kids and in the middle of a divorce. Or maybe you're like I was – doing good for everybody else but not doing well yourself. Sooner or later in life, we all have what I call a "What the heck?" moment. A moment when you take a good hard look at your life and incredulously ask yourself, "When did my life become *this*?" And if you keep staring long enough, you'll probably ask yourself this even scarier question, "And what if 'this' is all there is?"

Regardless of our age, level of education or societal status, if we're not careful, we all run the risk of living somebody else's life, experiencing that "what the heck" moment.

Funny thing is, as I stared at the emergency room walls I realized that this wasn't my first "what the heck" experience. I'd been here before. Physically exhausted, nerves frayed, emotionally and mentally drained. While I was doing incredibly meaningful work, I still found myself not only battling depletion on a few fronts, but also fighting a lack of fulfillment. But this wasn't my first rodeo. Five years prior, I'd found myself in a very similar predicament. Different place, different role, different people, but same outcome.

Now I realized that the reason I was back at square one wasn't because I wasn't intelligent enough, driven enough, capable enough, spiritual enough, or even attractive enough. The reason I was once again stuck had absolutely nothing to do with my career path, other people, or even timing. I was stuck again in an unhealthy professional situation because, deep down I continued to hold onto limiting beliefs and paradigms. Not only weren't these things serving me well, they were actually killing me. Obviously I survived that harrowing trip to the ER, but my soul was dying.

In my forty-nine years on earth, I'd spent almost thirty of them working in professional roles in finance, law and ministry, eventually working my way up to executive leadership roles in both the profit and non-profit sectors. These roles were exactly what I had spent my life preparing for. So why had I found myself frustrated, unfulfilled, and unhappy? Why were they not what I really wanted when they should have been?

I'd spent most of my twenties and thirties feeling duty-bound to stick with the career I had invested so much time and money in – practicing law. I was making a great living. But I wasn't alive. I felt as if I was meant for something greater, although I wasn't sure what that "greater" should be.

Ever since I was five or six years old, I've had an unshakeable sense that I wasn't supposed to be average. That my life was supposed to be bigger than what it was. I had a feeling that would one day, somehow, the words I spoke would have an indelible impact on people's lives. Monique Carkum's voice would be significant!

But my young life had its fair share of dissonance. While I was a pretty bright kid who could perform well in the classroom, at my core I was shy and self-conscious, never feeling comfortable in the spotlight. I could push myself academically (with two parents who were educators, I didn't have much choice), but I never felt comfortable putting myself out there in other ways. I was easily embarrassed and hated to try new things, especially in front of other people. Although I loathed speaking in front of an audience, I was raised in a southern, black baptist church full of educators. This meant Sunday school lessons had to be delivered with oratory precision and reading the church announcements was an Olympic sport. So who ended up delivering her fair share of those despite terrible stage fright? You guessed it – me.

I could never quite reconcile the feeling that I was born to have a voice with my tendency to run and hide from being noticed or my fear of trying new things. So I stuck to what I was relatively good at – academics. As a junior in college and a new Christian, I decided becoming a lawyer would be the vehicle by which my words would impact others' lives. By the time I was practicing law in my mid-twenties, I had a strong sense I was supposed to live a vibrant, dynamic life and help others do the same. But still I had no clue what that really meant and zero insight for how to go about doing it. So I spent my thirties working grueling hours in a career I could barely stand on a good day. While as a corporate lawyer I enjoyed the proximity to business strategy, structuring transactions and deal negotiations, I found the practice of law and the attention to detail it demanded tedious and boring most of the time. Why did I stay?

I was raised by two African-American, masters degree-holding parents who were married with kids before the "white only" signs were taken down in New Orleans. I wasn't raised to think about feeling alive and dynamic. Curtis and Bernice Carkum raised me to get an education so I could make a good living and take advantage of all the career opportunities they were denied even with advanced education. As a corporate lawyer in a Fortune 100 company, I was living my parents' dream. Couple that with a gigantic student loan bill and absolutely no idea how to figure out my next move, and I felt stuck. Having a "good job" and making a good living is what I was familiar with, and yet uncomfortable and unfulfilled in.

But trying to suppress the feeling that I was created for more was like trying to hold a beach ball underwater. It never worked for long. As I soldiered forward in my career, little five-year-old Monique kept popping up to the surface, whispering, "But weren't you supposed to change people's lives with your words?"

By the time I surveyed my life in my mid-thirties, what I once had hopes of being, giving and accomplishing had almost disintegrated under the weight of fear and conformity. My dream of living a vibrant life and doing engaging and meaningful work had been gagged, bound, and shoved into the trunk of obligation and driven off to Mediocre City, with busyness behind the wheel and guilt riding shotgun in the passenger seat.

My life – my God-given purpose, the vitality that comes from operating in that purpose and the impact God wanted to have on others' lives through me – had been hijacked.

While practicing law, I realized I needed an outlet to do meaningful work 'cause my day job wasn't cutting it. As believers in Christ, my husband Lennon and I had always been active in our local church, so it provided the perfect environment in which to contribute. For years we served in church leadership, created and led ministries, organized and oversaw events, taught in Christian education and preached. I found fulfillment watching people's lives be transformed by the power of the gospel of Jesus Christ. I absolutely loved helping people see possibilities beyond their current reality and raising their expectations for the kind of life they should be living. And most of all, I loved doing it through God's Word. Through these opportunities to serve, I had a chance to identify and hone some of my talents that weren't being utilized in my legal career.

However, there were some things I did enjoy as a corporate attorney. One benefit to being a senior executive at a Fortune 100 company was exposure to some of the best leadership and management development training there was. For years, I sat in annual operating reviews and strategic planning sessions imagining how the same rigor and process excellence could be used to advance God's kingdom. Year after year, I had a growing sense that God wanted me to invest what I was learning in the development of Christian leadership and the local church's operational competencies.

By the time I entered my forties, I had a much clearer idea of what I was called to do and thought the nonprofit sector, particularly local church ministry, would be a better fit for me. But while I was encouraging others to make bold moves and "step out in faith," deep down I wasn't much of a risk taker. Leaving my very-well-paying career while Lennon was starting his own law firm felt like I was playing high stakes poker in Vegas. Exciting, but not too smart.

I fought it for a while, wondering if ministry was what I was supposed to pursue but fearful of misreading the "signs." But when God wants us to move and we don't, He knows how to give us a loving shove in the right direction. God allowed a life-changing event (which I share in detail in Chapter 10) to spark my transition. Thrilled to be part of something bigger than myself and a mission more important than dollars and cents, I jumped into full-time ministry with both feet. I was excited to be part of something so significant in the lives of others, both here on earth and eternally. Working in the local church also meant I'd finally get to fulfill what for years I'd thought God wanted me to do - put my leadership and management experience to work for God's kingdom.

But after several years, here I was yet again, living but still not feeling fully alive. In pursuing good for others, I neglected to pay attention to what was healthy for me. Anyone involved in full-time ministry generally, and pastoring in particular, can attest to the stresses of caring for people spiritually and emotionally. After working endlessly to meet others' needs, I'd finally reached a breaking point as I sat in the ER.

In Christian theology, a person's soul consists of her mind, will, and emotions. I've always been a mentally tough, strong-willed person who could soldier through even in the face of challenging circumstances. Yes, the long hours that my pastoral role demanded left me physically and emotionally exhausted. But truth be told, it wasn't just my physical body that wasn't healthy. My soul was dying.

Yes, I was part of a team with an incredible mission serving wonderful people whom I loved dearly. But after several years I began to feel not only physically tired, but also restless once again. I felt obligated to stay in a role that, while fulfilling on many levels for the first couple years, ultimately failed to fully utilize the management and leadership skills I'd been blessed to acquire over the years in Corporate America. I felt called to an organizational culture that placed limitations on my potential because of gender, among other things, and therefore not so subtly implied that I should shrink to fit. And as someone who loves learning and developing professionally, I felt frustrated by the dearth of growth opportunities and mentorship in my current environment. Even though I was surrounded by terrific parishioners I still felt, in a word, stagnant. I was so busy *doing* that I'd been existentially kidnapped once again without even realizing it.

How in the world did I end up here? Especially since I'd already experienced the same struggle in my previous career? Truth is, I had no one to blame but me. Only this time, it blindsided me with harsher consequences. Suffering from physical and emotional burnout, a doctor-mandated medical leave of several weeks gave me the time and space I desperately needed to self-reflect. I prayed and thought long and hard as I learned to, as my kids say, "master the art of doing nothing."

THE SNATCH BACK: RECLAIMING YOUR LIFE ONE TRUTH AT A TIME

With what I realized was a gift of self-reflective and healing time, I understood three things were primarily responsible for my high-jacked existence: (1) my internal thoughts—the mistaken self-talk I'd allowed myself to believe, (2) how I had chosen to invest my time, and ultimately, (3) my lack of trust in God. As I looked at each of those issues, I realized the only common denominator was me. Which was *great* news, because that's the only factor I had any control over.

Once God made that real to me, and I submitted my will to His leadership, my whole life began to shift in a matter of weeks. My physical energy increased dramatically, my sleep patterns improved, my joy factor rose exponentially, and I began to radiate a vitality that was downright contagious. I mean contagious as in twerking-in-my-kitchen-when-no-one-was-watching, second-lining[1]-to-my car-in-the-shopping-mall-parking-lot, cracking-jokes-with-random-people in-the-grocery-store!

Settling for an Average Life?

What made the difference? A simple passage from the New Testament. While speaking to a crowd, Jesus said, "The thief's purpose is to steal and

---

[1] Google if you aren't from New Orleans.

kill and destroy. My purpose is to give them a rich and satisfying life."[2]

The life Jesus came to give us is anything but mediocre. And it's the

antithesis of overwhelming and stressful.

Jesus came to give us a life that is chock-full of purpose, brimming

with vitality, and overflowing with impact. On a scale of one to ten, this

rich and satisfying life that Jesus offers us is a mind-blowing twenty. But

let me be absolutely clear: this rich and satisfying John 10:10 life isn't a

repackaging of the played-out health and wealth prosperity gospel. This

abundant life isn't completely void of money troubles or health problems.

And it's not a self-absorbed, responsibility-free nirvana.

The John 10:10 preferred life that Jesus has for us is one that uses

the gifts and talents God's given us in a way that has an eternal impact for

His kingdom. It's the fulfillment of God's plan and purpose for our lives

that makes our lives rich and satisfying. The John 10:10 life Jesus

promised us is one defined by fully embracing that purpose, abundant with

God's joy, rest, peace and power. And until we can honestly describe

---

[2] John 10:10, NEW LIVING TRANSLATION

every aspect of our lives this way, we're living beneath our privilege as children of God.

I'd read John 10:10 so often throughout my life that I could recite it in my sleep. But knowing and doing are two drastically different things. We've often heard the phrase, *"If you know better, you'll do better."* When it came to John 10:10, I knew better, but I wasn't doing better. The bridge between knowing and doing is paved right thinking, smart investments of our time and carefully placed trust.

During my quiet time on medical leave, I began to really meditate on John 10:10, not just quote it. I began to wholeheartedly embrace that Jesus has a preferred life for me—not just in eternity but right here, right now. I thought of the mantra I'd learned in grade school: "Good. Better. Best. Never let it rest until your good is better, and your better is best!" I began to evaluate every area of my life and assess whether it was good, better, or best. Did my life reflect abundance and satisfaction as Jesus would define it? Was I living the best life Jesus came to give me? Too often my evaluation uncovered good, but average. I clearly knew one thing: I didn't want to be average. And I didn't believe God wanted that for me either. But I knew someone who did.

In John 10:10, Jesus also talks about the thief. This thief comes not to give life, but to take it. To steal life, kill it, and destroy it. This thief is the enemy of our souls, Satan. And he will stop at nothing to keep us from experiencing the life Jesus promised could be ours—a rich and satisfying life full of purpose, vitality, and impact. If he can't make our lives miserable, he's just as happy to make us wallow in the depths of being average, of giving in to mediocrity. Satan's job is the antithesis of Jesus'. And from the looks of things—as I could attest during my medical leave— he was doing his job extremely well. I'd fallen asleep to the reality of that thief and had allowed myself to become so overwhelmed with the pursuit of what I thought was God's plan that I lost my way.

I know I'm not the only one who has struggled with this. From young adults to baby boomers, I speak constantly with people who are fighting to find and live out their purpose. No wonder Rick Warren's *The Purpose Driven Life* is one of the bestselling books of all time. But instead of a best or preferred life, many of us are experiencing average.

And it's not for a lack of trying. Whenever someone would ask me how I was doing, my go-to response was the truth: "I'm so busy" or "I'm exhausted." Recognizing that truth, I realized that I was living in such a way that purpose, vitality, and impact was being slowly sucked out of my life, even though I was feverishly occupying my time with very good things—ministry, family, social and church activities - all things that should have brought the elusive fulfillment I desired.

It's been said that when given the opportunity to do as they please, most people usually choose to imitate someone else. And the more people doing "it," the more that choice is validated in our minds. In other words, "monkey see, monkey do" and the more monkeys doing it, the more other monkeys want to do it, too. And it, whatever it is, becomes the norm. Funny how we humans are. We've normalized a frenetic, unfulfilling pace that few of us, if any, truly enjoy. Humans' amazing ability to adapt is a great skill for surviving, but not for thriving.

Becoming over-scheduled is practically an adult rite of passage. Sure, the practical demands of life dictate that we often must prioritize productivity over leisure. Yes, we must be adults. But too often I'd mistaken busyness for productivity and confused career with calling. Perhaps you have too? We get so accustomed to being busy and existing in a state of perpetual overwhelm that our lives are plundered by the enemy of our souls.

Our "under-purposed," over-scheduled, unfulfilled lives are often a result of having settled for survival at some point, of having settled for an average life. It's as if our rich, satisfying lives have been stolen, and the robbery was ever so subtle. If the enemy launched a full-on, in-your-face, frontal attack, we'd wake up and fight back. But Satan is patient and cunning, his thievery gradual. He gets us to drop our guard by convincing us that average is okay. And we're so overworked, stressed, and exhausted that, frankly, average sounds fine, easier, and even desirable. By the time the enemy's done, we're left with a stripped existence that becomes the version of life that we ultimately accept, leaving a legacy devoid of the kind of impact and influence God planned for us to have.

Time to Snatch Back Our Lives

When I came out of that medical leave, I came out with renewed mind. My beliefs, my self-talk, my insecurities—everything that I'd held onto was no longer going to hold me hostage. I was no longer going to allow someone else's expectations to dictate my role or purpose. I was going to follow God's guidance, knowing who I was and who I was meant to be, and I wasn't going to go back to the way things had been. I was ready to buck the system. A little rebellion is good for the soul. Rebellion against the dictates of cultural and societal pressures, that is.

So I decided to draw a line in the proverbial sand and not allow the tide of life to wash away my purpose any longer. I was going to fight against the lies I'd believed for too long. I was no longer going to allow stress and overwork to dictate my life. I was no longer going to be okay with average. I was going to snatch back my life.

When I made that decision and began to pursue who I was meant to be, the most amazing things happened. I've never again found myself in that stressed-out, overworked, unfulfilled spot. I've found peace and contentment, joy and fulfillment. And every day, I keep pursuing and learning and influencing others to be their best as well. And I'm not looking back.

It's time for you to do the same. It's time for you to snatch back what the thief has stolen from you. Have you read my experience and found yourself relating to the ache, the frustration, and unfulfilled desires you've long had? Imagine refusing to settle for anything less than that rich and satisfying John 10:10 kind of life. Think about the lives you'd impact and the vitality you'd exude as you fulfill the purpose God has for you. I can tell you with 100 percent certainty, that's the kind of life that won't ever make you look back in longing or wondering.

This is why I wrote *The Snatch Back*. You and I are going to walk this journey together as we identify and break unhealthy norms in the areas of our thoughts, time, and trust so we can live the preferred, rich and satisfying life God created us to and to. Together, we're going to *thrive, not merely survive.*

I entitled this book *The Snatch Back,* not *The Request* or *The Pretty Please, Can I Have It Back?* Why? Because life circumstances and the enemy of our souls aren't going to sit idly by and allow us to skip blissfully unchallenged into the preferred life God has for us. After all, we read the enemy's job description in John 10:10: "The thief's purpose is to steal and kill and destroy." The enemy wants to steal our purpose, kill our vitality, and destroy our impact. He didn't come to play. So neither should you nor I.

The word *snatch* means to quickly seize something in a rude or eager way. Don't get it twisted: you will have to *forcibly* take back your thoughts, your time and your trust from things that will continue to rob you as long as you let them. When it comes to obtaining your preferred

John 10:10 life, politeness is overrated. In fact, politeness will get you killed. You're in a fight for your life with the enemy of your soul. And I've never seen a polite fight. Politeness might make you popular, but it won't get you your life back. In this life, *you don't get what you deserve; you get what you fight for and you'll end up with whatever you settle for*. So it's time to stop clutching your pearls. You have to knuckle up to get your preferred life back from the clutches of mediocrity.

In the following pages, I want to embolden you to go after your John 10:10 life and snatch it back, without a "please" or a "may I" in sight. In this book you'll explore your thoughts, time and trust - the same three areas I had to address to establish and live in my preferred life. You'll take a good hard look at some ingrained thought patterns and learn how to reclaim your mind from stinkin' thinkin'. You'll learn to cherish the time God has given you here on earth and learn strategies for how to take back control in order to maximize it. And you'll examine some of the stumbling blocks that keep you from trusting God, others, and yourself, and what you can do to live free of fear and uncertainty.

Throughout this book, you'll likely find yourself wanting to take notes and record your reactions, as well as complete the exercises I've included

21

under the heading "Do Your Work." To facilitate this, I've developed

"The Snatch Back Notebook," a free resource filled with practical prompts

and plenty of space for you to work out how to apply these concepts to

your life. To download the free notebook, visit

moniquecarkumedwards.com/tsbnotebook.

A rich and satisfying future is waiting for you. It's time for a snatch

back. So let's go!

Chapter 1

Taken

The 2009 movie *Taken* features actor Liam Neeson as former spy and trained assassin Bryan Mills and Bryan's estranged seventeen-year-old daughter, Kim. Over her father's objections, Kim and a friend travel alone to Paris for vacation. Horrifically, Kim and her friend are abducted by sex traffickers shortly after arriving. This movie depicts every parent's worst nightmare and is the singular reason our daughter, Brooklynn, will still be traveling with her father when she's thirty-two.

Prior to Kim leaving home Bryan gives her the typical "don't talk to strangers" safety speech. Despite all of her father's warnings, Kim lets her guard down and makes a new male acquaintance in Paris, who unbeknownst to Kim, is working with sex traffickers to abduct unsuspecting young women. After being tipped off to the girls' location by this acquaintance, the kidnappers break into the girls' apartment, first abducting Kim's friend. As Kim hides under a bed, she frantically calls her father back in the United States. "Now, the next part is very important," Bryan tells Kim as he directs what she needs to do. "They are going to take you. Kim, *stay focused.*"

With just a few days until Kim will be auctioned off as a sex slave and the kidnappers unwilling to release her, Bryan goes on a killing spree, sparing no one until he rescues his daughter. Besides being stunned and impressed by Bryan's assassin skills, I spent the next hour and a half imagining what it must be like to be threatened with the loss of something so precious and irreplaceable—life itself.

Despite all her father's safety admonitions, Kim allowed herself to be distracted and disarmed by a new, very attractive male acquaintance. She dropped her guard, got too comfortable with someone who seemed friendly enough, but ended up being potentially lethal. In life, we get comfortable – lulled into the routine, satisfied with the attractive but mediocre, or distracted by the challenges of everyday life. We drop our guard, forgetting we have a very real enemy whose job number one is to steal our purpose, kill our vitality and destroy our impact during our time on this earth. The result: a kidnapped existence. One that leaves you living a life far beneath the rich and satisfying life Jesus promised in John 10:10.

I don't know about you, but I hate being promised something and then not getting it. I can't stand forfeiting something that could have very well been mine. Even as a corporate attorney negotiating deals, I hated leaving money on the table. If I thought my client should get it, I went after it. And rarely did I come back empty-handed.

Maybe you're the type of person that doesn't mind missing out, forfeiting, giving up. But something tells me you wouldn't have picked up this book if you were. I suspect you're ready to reclaim your life, full of all the purpose, vitality and impact you've imagined. But maybe you just don't know where to start. Or perhaps you're already on your way and need some encouragement as you journey forward.

My prayer is that this book will help spark your desire to go after the life Jesus promised you, spur your faith to believe it's possible and give you specific steps to propel your progress.

One Life to Live

Unlike Bryan who became immediately aware of the imminent threat to his daughter's safety, many of us endure an existence that kidnaps our minds, wills, and emotions - a crime that goes unnoticed. Subtle and cunning, the enemy of our souls conspires with life circumstances to rob

us of our purpose, hold our vitality hostage, and obliterate our impact.
Rarely does this happen forthrightly. If it did, most of us would
immediately recognize the invasion, feel the loss, and take some sort of
action in an attempt to minimize the damage. No, for most of us the
kidnapping of our existences comes without clear warning. Unlike Kim,
we don't have a Bryan to warn us about what will happen next. It's as if
we wake up one day with a life we didn't ask for, want, or recognize. Our
lives—precious and irreplaceable—have been snatched.

Indiscriminate in its target, life abduction can sneak up on the atheist,
the Christian, and everyone in between. While faith in Christ can certainly
help you reclaim your life, it doesn't exempt you from being existentially
kidnapped in the first place. Yes, you read that right: you can be "saved,
sanctified, filled with the Holy Ghost and fire-baptized"[3] and still get
jacked. Because the Snatch Back is less about the life to come, and more
about how you show up in the here and now, using in this life every bit of
what God gave you.

---

[3] If you know what this means, you are a certified "old skool" church head. Be proud.

In *Taken*, Bryan is faced with the potential loss of his one and only daughter. Remember that scene where he debated about whether to go after the kidnappers and try to recover Kim? Yeah, me neither. Didn't. Happen. Bryan valued his daughter beyond description and immediately recognized the significance of the threat. That recognition propelled Bryan into forceful, decisive action.

Do you realize what's at stake in your life – the one valuable, irreplaceable life God has given you? Author and pastor Louie Giglio says, "There's too much at stake to die with a small vision."[4] While I wholeheartedly agree with Louie, I'm here to reframe that and say there's too much at stake to *live* with a small vision.

The God who created this universe and all the wonders contained in it thought the universe needed a *you*. And He created you not just to worship Him, but to fulfill a divine purpose that couldn't be fulfilled by anybody else. If it could have been, He wouldn't have needed to create you. The one life you've been given is meant to be lived *in* purpose and *on* purpose.

---

[4] Louie Giglio, *Goliath Must Fall: Winning the Battle Against Your Giants,* 2017.

When He created you, God put a vision inside your heart. A valuable vision. The value of your vision can't be measured in dollar signs, number of followers, likes, tags, or media mentions. Your vision is valuable by virtue of the One who gave it to you. I don't care whether your purpose is to work for UNICEF, invent a disrupting technology, raise generous kids in a selfish world, or open an ice cream parlor—God gave you that vision, and it has immense value. It's the fuel that will propel you into your preferred John 10:10 life. Don't you dare let the enemy of your soul and life circumstances steal, kill, and destroy what God gave you. Take decisive action. Go after your preferred life just like Bryan went after Kim. Search for it, find it, and snatch it back!

It's A Matter of Life or Death

Once Kim was kidnapped, every second until her rescue was extremely precious. And just like Kim's rescue, there's no time to lose in reclaiming our lives. Enter Operation Snatch Back – the process by which we reclaim that John 10:10 life.

Operation Snatch Back is the intentional assessment of three key life domains: our thoughts, our time and our trust. It's the honest evaluation of where, in each of those three domains, we've allowed the enemy of our souls to convince us that settling for average is sufficient and that a rich and satisfying John 10:10 life is for some reason beyond our grasp.

Finally, Operation Snatch Back requires taking the bold steps necessary to reclaim our God-given life purpose, and the vitality and impact that flow as a result of living in purpose on purpose.

Maybe you're thinking: "Monique, lots of good people live average lives. What's so bad about settling for average?" Let's take another look at John 10:10. Jesus said, "The thief's purpose is to steal and kill and destroy. My purpose is to give them a rich and satisfying life." In many other passages Jesus makes his point by telling a parable or using hyperbole. But not here. In this verse, Jesus is saying what He means and means what He says: 'On the one hand, the devil's purpose is to steal, kill and destroy. On the other hand, my purpose is to give you a rich and satisfying life.' I don't read about a third hand. In other words, Jesus doesn't present an in-between option. Jesus doesn't say you can split the baby and settle for a nice comfortable average. No! Jesus is drawing a line in the sand – either you're down with His purpose-filled life or you can roll with the devil's plan to ultimately destroy you, so choose carefully.

Operation Snatch Back is a matter of life or death. It's a matter of living the preferred life God has for you, or watching the person you were meant to be die slowly and painfully. The choice is squarely yours. Nobody other than Jesus will ever care more about your God-given purpose than you do. Not your family, not your best friend, not your tribe, not your prayer partner, not your mastermind group. Sure other people will support, love, and encourage you. But none of them is going to fight as hard for your life as you should. Don't expect them to. It's your life, not theirs. It's your dream, not theirs. This. Is. All. On. You. If you want to live a life full of purpose, vitality, and impact, you have to become determined never to quit until the mission of snatching back your life is accomplished.

In the movie *Taken*, Bryan not only realizes the value of what has been kidnapped, but also he recognizes the fragility of what's been taken. Bryan's fully aware that with each passing minute, his chances of recovering Kim are diminished. So Bryan moves with unbelievable resolve and singular focus.

Law enforcement statistics tell us that the first twelve to twenty-four hours are the most crucial in a missing person's case. Why? Because as time elapses, clues disappear, trails grow cold, and witnesses' memories grow more blurry. The longer a person is missing, the lower the chances of a positive outcome, so an abducted life is indeed a fragile one.

Maybe you're thinking, "I hear you, Mo. But this really isn't a good time for me to snatch my life back. I mean, I've got so much going on right now. I'm going to deal with all this 'reclaiming my life' stuff another time." The future isn't promised to any of us, so all we have is the here and now. In the Old Testament, the psalmist writes "Teach us to use wisely all the time we have."[5] In the New Testament, Jesus told his disciples, "We must quickly carry out the tasks assigned us by the one who sent us. The night is coming, and then no one can work."[6] Over and over, Scripture admonishes us to make the most of the time we have and conveys we should have a sense of urgency in completing our God-given assignments.

Here's a different way of looking at it: perhaps your busyness is precisely the reason *to* initiate Operation Snatch Back. We can be busy,

---

[5] Psalms 90:12, Contemporary English Version
[6] John 9:4, New Living Translation

but not productive. We can be active, but have little real impact. Being too busy to pursue our preferred John 10:10 life means we're too busy to really live.

And waiting to reclaim your life certainly won't make the task any easier. The longer you wait, the less time you'll have, the fewer people you'll touch, and the more opportunity the enemy has to steal your purpose, kill your vitality and destroy your impact. That means waiting around for a better time to reclaim your life just isn't an option. Hear me clearly: your purpose dying is one too many, regardless of what it is. So Operation Snatch Back is about waking up and taking action. You have to do something about it. And soon.

What's the alternative? Settling. Settling for average, mundane. Settling for people pleasing over purpose, fear over faith. Maybe you're thinking, "Hey, settling doesn't sound so bad." Here's the gotcha: We think we're settling for the status quo, which often seems harmless, but settling is really just a form of slow death in disguise. Remember, in John 10:10 Jesus doesn't split the baby. It's either a preferred, God-inspired life or one that's been pillaged and looted by the enemy. There is no third hand. The status quo never stays the status quo. Like a building that's been abandoned, deterioration creeps in and takes over. From one day to the next the building looks fine - you can't tell that the elements are eating away at it. But come back a year later and you can see the damage. There's always a slow erosion that takes place imperceptibly.

My prayer for you is that your days of settling for a slow, imperceptible death are over. I have soaked the writing of this book in prayer for every single reader who will pick it up determined to reclaim their lives and live free. But the working of that freedom from concept to reality is going to take more than prayer. Scripture teaches that "all hard work brings a profit, but mere talk leads only to poverty."[7] All this "snatching back your life" stuff? There's a huge spiritual, mental, and emotional profit to be gained (and maybe even financial). But it takes *work*.

And what will you get in return for your trouble? A reclaimed, repurposed life that reflects God's preferred plan for your unique personality, gifts and talents. A life that exudes vitality and has a lasting

---

[7]Proverbs 14:23, New International Version

impact on others. A John 10:10 life. A Snatched Back life is indeed a rich

and satisfying one.

Chapter 2

It's Gonna Cost Ya

When I first decided to snatch my life back, I didn't fully appreciate how rewarding a reclaimed life would be, but I also underestimated how challenged I would feel in the process. For decades, I had led a diminished, play-it-safe existence, often constrained by my own limiting beliefs. It took me a while to make the mind-set shifts that would enable me to ultimately create a life of purpose, vitality, and impact. Before we embark upon the how-tos of snatching back your life, let me share with you the three most significant mind-set shifts that fueled my transformation. Adopting these will be crucial in successfully executing your own Operation Snatch Back.

Mind-set Shift #1: Prepare to Pay Up

In 2004, when the nationwide real estate market was booming, Lennon and I purchased an investment property in Virginia. We fixed it up, found an incredibly reliable tenant, kicked back, and watched the rent checks roll in. Things went great for several years until the bottom fell out of the real estate market, our equity in the property evaporated, and the property went underwater financially.

Over time, our investment property desperately needed an overhaul, but given the distance and other issues, major renovations weren't an option. We eventually decided to get rid of it, but every time we tried to sell it the offers were less than what we owed the bank. We kept delaying the inevitable, but in the meantime we still had all the expenses and hassles of owning the property. And as much as we hated all that, the prospect of having to cough up money at closing was too painful for us. Until...

Until we got completely sick and tired of the tenants, phone calls, repairs, and all the other hassles of being a landlord. It was as if we woke up one day and decided enough was enough. Instead of being resentful about the money we'd have to pay at closing, we began to see it as a (not so) small price to pay for freedom and peace. Once our perspective changed, we began thanking God we had the financial means to pay it. The money we had in the bank represented the price of freedom. We could pay it and walk away from this investment, or we could decide to hold on to the property and continue to be miserable. We spent years griping about being bound by this investment-turned-sour, but we weren't willing to pay the price to get free.

Freedom always costs something. Wars are waged and blood is shed when a nation's freedom is threatened. Civil rights icons like Medgar Evers worked tirelessly so African-Americans could have the ability to vote like other Americans—and he died because of it. Jesus Christ died so that those who place their faith in Him can experience freedom from the bondage of sin. Regardless of whether it's democracy, civil rights, or eternity, freedom always costs. Operation Snatch Back is about reclaiming your life from the things that have robbed your life of its purpose, vitality, and impact. The Snatch Back is freedom and peace. And it's going to cost you.

In order to reclaim your life, you must be willing to embrace this mind-set shift: *If you don't sacrifice for the life you want, the life you want becomes the sacrifice.* As an executive strategist, I work with professional people of faith who want to amplify their impact in their work environments. My clients desire to use the gifts God has given them to the fullest. For many of my clients, their desired life will require a major transformation in their thinking, belief systems, and time expenditures.

Many people know me as a preacher, speaker, or facilitator—roles in which I do most of the talking. But as an executive strategist, I assume the roles of coach, consultant, and guide, requiring me to listen way more than I speak. On this journey of transformation, my work is client-led and deeply personal, therefore I listen intently to my clients' feelings, desires, and goals. After understanding and digesting these, my clients' responses to the next two questions are critical: How badly do you want this transformation? And what are you willing to sacrifice to achieve it?

When asked to rate how badly they want the desired transformation on a scale of one to ten (ten being "I want this more than life itself"), most clients will say an eight or nine. Makes sense because, after all, they're spending their hard-earned coins to hire me. But the dissonance bubbles up when I ask them to bring to our next session the list of all the things they're willing to *sacrifice* in order to achieve said desired transformation.

I've had clients return with a blank sheet of paper, at which point I happily refund their money because, while they are indeed lovely (all my clients are), they are simply not ready for transformation. I've had other clients list everything from sleep to social media to sex, and mean it. *Those* clients are my people.

In embracing this mindset shift, it's critical that you identify what you are willing to give up so you can snatch your life back. What are you willing to sacrifice to live free? Take some time to really think and pray about this.

A starter list of things to sacrifice might include:

- The need to be right

- Social acceptance/status

- Your image

- A dream borne out of ego

- The desire to make everyone else happy

- Avoiding necessary, healthy conflict to "keep the peace"

- Steady paycheck/financial security

- Time with acquaintances

Please don't just read this list. Get out a pen and paper and create your own list. In The Snatch Back Notebook, you'll find space dedicated to writing responses to this and the "Do Your Work" prompts throughout this book.[8]

When you list something you're willing to sacrifice, really drill down on it. Ask yourself: What's been its significance in my life? What would giving this up look like in my everyday life? What will I gain from sacrificing this? How will its departure from my life help me snatch back my purpose, vitality and impact?

In executing my own Operation Snatch Back, I had to grapple with the concept of calling. I had served in church leadership in various volunteer capacities since I was nineteen years old. I finally had answered "yes" to what I believed was a holy calling. The thought that I might disappoint God by walking away from this vocationally was tormenting for me at times. One of the things I had to sacrifice was the familiarity of working in church ministry and the approval it brought from others. I was also torn over giving up what many see as the pinnacle of church leadership – full-time pastoring. Folks were so happy for me when I became a full-time pastor. What would they think of me walking away from it now? As a

---

[8] You can download the free notebook at
www.moniquecarkumedwards.com/tsbnotebook.

pastor, I was highly relational and over time many of the church members became my friends and some were actual relatives. Working full-time as a pastor, my professional, social and spiritual worlds all meshed together creating relationships and interconnections that can be difficult to untangle and separate, and yet still keep intact. Could I move forward without fracturing these?

But my Operation Snatch Back involved more than just transitioning out of ministry. I also had to wrestle with something bigger – the fear of moving totally outside my comfort zone. As an executive strategist, speaker and writer, I'm now an entrepreneur, and therefore the face of my company. I am my brand. This may not seem like a big deal to you, but deep down in some ways I was still that self-conscious little girl who hated being the center of attention. I was fearful of being rejected, judged, critiqued and criticized by people. What if no one wanted to hire me as their career coach? What if no one showed up to hear me speak? What if I wrote this book and my mama and Lennon were the only ones who bought a copy?

When I was a pastor, Jesus and the Gospel were center stage. If someone rejected or criticized what I had to say, I didn't take it personally.

43

Hey, they were rejecting the message of Christ, not me. In ministry, the hours were long, the pay wasn't fabulous, the emotional toll could be costly and the working conditions weren't always ideal, but I could play small and hide.

However, now in this new role, I had to be willing to sacrifice the approval, emotional comfort and security that full-time ministry had provided me and step out into the unknown, be front and center.

Remember: freedom is never free - it always costs you something. The question is whether you're prepared to pay up. As author Rachel Hollis says, "When you really want something, you will find a way. When you don't really want something, you'll find an excuse."[9] My own Operation Snatch Back caused me to be honest with myself about whether I wanted a way or an excuse.

For years, Lennon and I moaned about our investment property gone bad, but failed to take any action because we just didn't want to pay the price of selling. We used excuse after excuse to avoid making a tough decision. But when we finally wanted freedom badly enough, we coughed

---

[9] Rachel Hollis, *Girl, Wash Your Face: Stop Believing the Lies About Who You Are So You Can Become Who You Were Meant to Be*, 2018.

up the money (thank God we had it) and sold that sucker during the writing of this book. The day I went to the bank to wire the necessary closing funds, the banker obviously thought we were purchasing the home and gave me a big congratulations. The old me would have felt obligated to clarify that no, we weren't the buyers, we were actually the sellers who owed more money on the house than it was worth, blah, blah, blah. Instead, I gave him a big cheesy grin, and said "Thanks!" and walked out. Operation Snatch Back also frees you from unnecessary explanations.

Mind-set Shift #2: Find Your People

Whenever we do something contrary to the status quo, we run the risk of others misunderstanding us. Sometimes the steps we have to take to reclaim our lives can seem pretty radical. When we begin to snatch our lives back, not everyone will understand, celebrate, or support us. Our Snatch Back can be jarring to them.

Some people have never known you in any other season of your life. They're used to the current edition of you and they're good with you just as you are, thank you very much. Others may feel threatened when you begin snatching your life back. Perhaps your compromised life served them in some way or made them more comfortable with themselves.

When others observe you proactively reclaiming your life, they may become unsettled with their own hijacked existence. Still others may be jarred by your life changes because they've never known you to show up in any other way.

Your transformation may have them wondering, "Who *is* this new person?" And let's face it, unfortunately, some people are committed to misunderstanding you, no matter how much you try to explain. Regardless of the reason, before you can reclaim your life you have to accept that others may not celebrate your snatch back—and since they aren't God, that's completely okay. You don't need their permission or cooperation, because Operation Snatch Back is about *you*, not them.

But as you reclaim your life, you will need to feel supported. So take note of who isn't clapping. Don't villainize them in your mind, post subliminal messages about them on social media, or do anything else petty and unchristlike. Just quietly notice and then proceed to snatch your life back anyway. Transforming your life is hard work and you will need a lot of love and encouragement from others. The last thing you need is to look to someone for support who just can't or won't give it. So, notice who isn't clapping. Definitely still love and pray for them, just don't lean on 'em.

I often tell my clients on the road to living their preferred life, "Find companions if you can, but walk alone if you must." As they start to walk alone, they inevitably find others on the same road who can share and celebrate what God is doing in their lives. God created us to be in community with others, so I don't subscribe to the whole "It's just me, myself, and I" philosophy (which itself is often rooted in emotional hurt). We undoubtedly need other people. *But remember: you had a God-given purpose before anyone else had an opinion.* So it's awesome to have others celebrate you, but don't look to them to validate you.

In executing my Operation Snatch Back, I made a huge career change from being a pastor to becoming an executive strategist, speaker and author. Given how revered the pastoral office is in most Christian circles, I definitely got the side-eye of disapproval from a few folks who just didn't get it. Even my own mama was like, "Baby, are you *sure?*"

Some people questioned whether my decision was motivated by money and prestige (side note: if I was truly motivated by either of those things I never would have left my career as a corporate lawyer to become a pastor in the first place). My initial reaction: "Girl/Boy, bye." I was hurt because I thought they should have known me better than that. But God had to pull my card and remind me that at times I've misunderstood people, so I just needed to forgive them and move on. I also had to accept that some people simply couldn't give what they didn't have. It's hard to celebrate someone else's freedom when you're bound by the need for acceptance from other people. It's hard to embrace someone else's potential and possibility when you're stuck. The inability to understand or celebrate what God was doing in my life didn't make them bad people, they just weren't *my* people for this season of my life.

In life, we choose what to focus our attention on, and whatever we focus on expands. So we must choose wisely. While some didn't get or approve of the moves I was making, God did bless me with an incredible tribe of people who believed in and supported me. My sister Shelly, a fellow entrepreneur whose business acumen is phenomenal, encouraged and strategized with me almost daily. A few of my besties, Sylvia, Carmen, Debveda and Maryline, prayed for me, cheered me on, and bothered me about whether I was writing consistently. Others opened their networks to help me and sent clients my way.

It was my choice whether to focus on them or on the relative few who just didn't get it. So I made the decision to be effusively thankful e'ry daggone day for the people supporting me. Those were my people, and I chose to focus on them and thank God for what they brought into my life.

As you ease on down Snatch Back Road, keep going until you find your people. Then be thankful everyday for them.

Mind-set Shift #3: Find Your Signal

In science or engineering, signal-to-noise ratio is a measurement used to compare the power of a desired signal to the power of background noise. A ratio higher than 1:1 indicates more signal than noise.[10] Conversely, a ratio lower than 1:1 indicates more noise than signal. Signal-to-noise ratio can also be used metaphorically to refer to the ratio of meaningful, correct information to false or irrelevant information. In our lives we need to be mindful of the signal-to-noise ratio at any given moment. But how do we know what our signal is? How do we distinguish it from the noise?

---

[10]Signal-to-noise ratio. (n.d.) In Lexico's dictionary. Retrieved from https://www.lexico.com/en/definition/signal-to-noise_ratiohttps://www.lexico.com/en/definition/signal-to-noise_ratio

I define the signal in my life as God's purpose for my life: to be spiritual C-4 blowing the roof off possibilities for myself and others. I'm a disruptive force, challenging people to think higher, see bigger, and believe greater. Regardless of my role, title, career, or circumstances, spiritual C-4 is how I'm supposed to be showing up—it's who God has called me to be. In order to consistently do this, I have to adopt the mind-set that *anything that interferes with me being who God is calling me to be and living my preferred life is damaging noise that must be eliminated.*

When my thoughts are plagued with fear and doubt (noise) or I'm distrustful of God's timing (more noise), my actions don't line up with my purpose. When those things happen, I'm blocked by the noise from being who God called me to be. For instance, I delayed launching my speaking career because I battled with the noise of "Who, other than church folks, will ever come to hear me speak?" I knew I had a message to share beyond the church walls, but fear and insecurity kept me from really pursuing it. Five year old Monique, who believed she would one day impact people with her words, kept looking at grown Monique like "Girl, we don't have time for this!"

Even after embracing that I was called to impact both secular and sacred audiences, I would still battle with periods of doubt and reticence. This wasn't just a minor inconvenience. This kept me stuck in neutral - hidden, ineffective and playing small. It wasn't until I began the daily practice of reading and praying over my life purpose statement (more on that later in this chapter) that I started making consistent progress toward my speaking career. That life purpose statement is my signal, and knowing my signal keeps me focused and accountable. My signal acts like a siren, calling me back when I'm lost or beginning to drift.

I've worked with clients to discover their purpose, get a promotion and a huge raise. Trust me, they were more excited about discovering their purpose than the coins. I've had other clients take a significant pay cut in order to live out their purpose on purpose. There's something about knowing why God created you that makes you walk a little taller, smile a little brighter, and serve others more wholeheartedly. Money can't buy that.

While your life purpose isn't your decision, it's certainly your discovery. Accompanying clients on this journey of discovery is one of the most fulfilling things I do as a coach. People who know their purpose and step into it fully have a vitality that shows up in their actions and creates a lasting impact on the people around them.

Your life purpose is your signal. If you don't know your life purpose, spend some time praying and meditating about it, read one of the many great books on the subject, speak with your pastor or hire a life coach. Whether you call it audible spam or just a plain ole distraction, whatever interferes with the signal is noise. This world is a cacophony of stimuli coming from a chorus of discordant voices. Translation: there's a whole lotta distracting noise out there.

The purpose of snatching back your life is to help you eliminate the noise that's muffling your signal. If you're going to snatch your life back successfully, I'm going to need you to recognize the noise and put it on block like an ex you never want to hear from again. But that process starts with knowing your signal.

In Section 2 of The Snatch Back Notebook there is a series of questions designed to help you discover or refine your life purpose. Once you've written your life purpose statement, let that be the signal that calls you out of mediocrity and into the rich, satisfying preferred life God has for you. Everything else is just noise.

This book is divided into three sections based on the inner work that I and many of my clients have had to do to reclaim their lives and live with purpose, vitality and impact. Let's head over to Section One, where we'll explore the foundation of Operation Snatch Back - the critical work of reclaiming your thoughts.

Chapter 3

Mind Your Mind

T his'll never work. I think I want to use our next couple of sessions to start brainstorming my exit strategy," said Kimberly[11], one of my executive coaching clients. A senior associate at a prominent boutique law firm, Kimberly is extremely capable and well-regarded. She's routinely placed on her firm's large, high-profile deals as the lead attorney, consistently produces outstanding results for clients and does a great job of managing and developing junior associates.

Despite being highly regarded by the firm's partners and beloved by her clients, Kimberly had convinced herself she had no future at the firm because she didn't "fit the mold" of the typical firm partner. So convinced was Kimberly that she'd never make it to the corner office, she came to me looking to transition out of her legal career altogether. I listened to Kimberly's story, and the more we talked the more I realized

---

[11] Client names have been changed throughout to protect privacy.

just how much goodness she had at her current gig - real sponsorship from

a couple of powerful firm partners, high visibility client assignments and

team loyalty. Kimberly had tons she could leverage, so why the fatalistic

outlook?

Ever think about your thoughts? If you think that's a weird

question, the answer's probably no. Our thoughts have the power to sink

us into despair or propel us into euphoria. Our thoughts have the power to

fill us with hope or drain us of all possibility. *Our thoughts influence our*

feelings, our feelings influence our actions, and our actions determine the

results with which we live. The degree to which this sequence is played

out in our lives varies from person to person depending on things like our

life experiences, disposition, emotional intelligence and discipline. But in

the end, we're all ultimately under the influence of our thoughts. Like a

guy who's consumed way too much liquor but is too drunk to realize it,

we stumble under the influence of our thoughts 24/7, mainly oblivious to

their impact. Facing the hangover of fractured relationships, messed up

finances, derailed careers and malnourished spirits, we hold our heads,

take two painkillers of blaming other people and somehow manage to do it

all over again and again. Time after time.

Don't believe me? Think about how every December 31st millions of people become filled with excitement at the prospect of what a new year will bring. Just the turning of a page on the calendar signals a fresh start. But in many instances we fail to move into what God has for us, regardless of what the calendar says, because while we say all the right things, old soundtracks are playing in our heads. While we've turned the page on the calendar, we haven't turned the corner in our *minds*.

And as a result, we stay stuck. Stuck on hurt. Stuck on what we think someone said about us. Stuck in pain. Stuck on failure. Stuck in fear. In some instances, stuck on stupid. And yet, many of us have a big vision for our lives - big things we want to see happen in us, through us, and for us. We have gifts that we want to invest in our families, our communities and the world at large. And since I believe each person is created in the image of an incredible God, there's absolutely nothing wrong with (and actually a lot right with) us having an extraordinary vision, an audacious goal, and incredible plans beyond where we are now. But there's an old expression, *"It's hard to be big when Little got you."*

And Little has some of us in his grip. All because we've allowed defeating, negative and unproductive thoughts to premier in the theater of

57

our minds. These overwhelming thoughts cast themselves in the starring role, take center stage and dominate our existence, causing us to live little. We talk big, but live small. We dream big, but live diminished. We talk about what could be, but still live in what used to be. And as a result Little has us because any "little" thing trips us up.

Ever got sidetracked behind someone else's opinion of you? Ever wasted valuable energy on a controversy with no real consequence? Ever spent months trying to convince yourself to settle for something that in your gut you knew just didn't feel right? Little got you, didn't he? Truth be told, he didn't just get you. He sucker-punched the daylights outta you and left you holding your head wondering, "What the heck . . .?" It's time to put the snatch on Little and while we're at it grab our minds and destinies back.

But where do you start? *One of the most dangerous things in the world is an unsupervised mind.* So let's start by paying attention to what you're paying attention to. I know, it sounds so basic it's hard to believe it actually works. But I challenge you to try it. It's been estimated that the

average person has between 12,000 and 60,000 thoughts per day.[12]
Research differs on whether these numbers represent conscious or
subconscious brain activity, but regardless that's a whole lotta thinking
going on! What's even more interesting is researchers estimate that almost
eighty percent of our thoughts are negative. And a whopping ninety-five
percent of our thoughts are the very same thoughts we had the day
before.[13] In short, we keep thinking the same ole defeatist thoughts day
after day. What in the world is up with that?

What's On Your Mind?

"For though we live in the world, we do not wage war as the world does.
The weapons we fight with are not the weapons of the world. On the
contrary, they have divine power to demolish strongholds. We demolish
arguments and every *pretension* that sets itself up against the knowledge
of God, and we take captive every *thought* to make it obedient to Christ."
2 Corinthians 10:3-5[14]

---

[12] Benjamin P. Hardy, PhD., "*To Have What You Want You Must Give Up What's Holding You Back,*" June 9, 2018, https://medium.com/the-mission/to-have-what-you-want-you-must-give-up-whats-holding-you-back-65275f844a5ald[13]

[14] New International Version, emphasis mine.

The Apostle Paul wrote these words to the church located in ancient Corinth, which was located in a major metropolis containing many of the vices of that day – drunkenness, adultery, prostitution, incest and fighting. In fact, Corinthians were known through the then-Roman empire for their immorality. You name it and the Corinthians were down with it. And unfortunately, but realistically, the same vices that were found in the city of Corinth were also found in the Corinthian church.

The Corinthian church's biggest problem seemed to be that although they were saved - they came up to the altar, said the sinners' prayer, joined the church and even came to church regularly – they seemed to be unable, perhaps unwilling, to divorce themselves from the culture around them.

To make matters worse, there were teachers who swooped down on the fledgling Corinthian church with erroneous doctrine designed to discredit Paul and ultimately pull the Corinthian believers away from the Gospel. And it's in the context of this ongoing controversy that Paul writes 2 Corinthians 10:3-5. Paul makes it clear he's not fighting against the false teachers. Paul is fighting against the false doctrines that have affected the Corinthians behavior.

But before doctrines and teachings can affect behavior, they have to take root in the heart. And before they lodge in the heart they have to take root in the mind - the thought life. Remember: Thoughts (the mind) influence feelings (the heart) which determine behavior (actions). This is why Romans 12:1-2 says, "Don't copy the behavior and customs of this world, but let God transform you into a new person by changing the way you *think*. Then you will learn to know God's will for you, which is good and pleasing and perfect.[15]" In other words, we change our lives by changing the way we think.

In the case of the Corinthians, wrong thoughts about the truth of the gospel created their problems. And for us today, our challenge is still wrong thoughts - thoughts that are contrary to how we should be thinking if we want to live lives of purpose, vitality and impact. If we actually pay attention to our thoughts, I'm pretty sure we'll find the vast majority of them have been molded by today's culture, just like the Corinthians' thoughts were shaped by the surrounding culture of their day. And not only are those thoughts often contrary to God's Word, they're just

---

[15] New Living Translation

downright unhelpful. Whether it's how we think about managing our relationships or our careers, raising our kids or investing our time, some of these thought patterns just don't serve us well at all. Whether it's the YOLO mindset that causes us to make reckless decisions today with little regard for their impact on tomorrow, or the "cancel culture" that encourages us to discard relationships instead of intentionally working on improving them, we're constantly bombarded by messages contrary to God's Word. We know this, and yet we still often say, believe and act on them.

The scriptures we just looked at from Romans & 2 Corinthians teach us that these thoughts represent ingrained patterns of thinking that impact our behavior. And to further explain this, in 2 Corinthians 10:3-5 Paul uses a metaphor of a stronghold to make his point. When Paul used the analogy of a "stronghold," the Corinthians immediately got it, although you might not. So let me explain.

What's A Stronghold?

As populations multiplied in ancient civilizations, people began to form organized communities, otherwise known as cities. The inhabitants of cities soon realized that living in the open allowed them to be victimized by invaders, who would attack and take control of defenseless cities. So city dwellers began putting walls around their territories, giving the inhabitants a source of protection, since potential invaders had to make their way through the city walls before they could conquer it. But soon builders of walled cities began to realize that walls not only made for good defense, but they also made for good offense. An army could launch an attack and then rest behind the city walls between offensive campaigns.

Strongholds were often located on a hilltop or a mountain, making it all the more difficult for their enemies to launch an attack against them because it's harder to fight going uphill (hence the idiom "uphill battle"). The army could launch attacks, and then retreat to the safety of its walled city. Thus, their point of operation became known as a "strong hold." And as this stronghold grew and prospered, it could then begin to exert control on the surrounding cities and villages, which were less secure.

Soon the city would grow and become known as a city-state. Eventually some of these city-states grew into nations; some would even become empires. But they all started out as a stronghold. One of the main objectives of an invading army was to take down the strongholds within a conquered territory. Because *if the stronghold remained, the territory was never truly conquered.*

And so it is with us - ingrained patterns of thinking in our minds can lead to spiritual strongholds. That spiritual stronghold is the devil's base of operation in our lives. Just like ancient armies used to do, the devil launches attacks against your spirit and then retreats behind this walled city. And it feels impossible to stop the onslaught. The enemy is constantly on the offensive against us and we're constantly on the defensive, just trying to live through the battle. No wonder instead of spiritually thriving we're often barely surviving. And yet Romans 8:37 says that we're not supposed to just be conquerors, but we're supposed to be *more than* conquerors.

You may know what it means to be a conqueror, but what in the world does it mean to be "more than a conqueror"? The phrase carries the idea of one that is unsurpassed, unequaled and unrivaled by any person or thing, and therefore in no real danger of loss, physical or otherwise.[16] In other words, we're supposed to be chillin'- showing up to the fight confident that we've got it on lock.

If this is the case, then why aren't we living as conquerors, let alone living as more than conquerors? Because we've allowed strongholds to remain. Remember: *if the stronghold remains intact, the territory is never truly conquered*! But how did the spiritual stronghold get there in the first place?

The devil is not a creator - only God is. But the devil is a builder. And what exactly does a builder do? A builder uses raw materials to construct something. A home builder takes two by fours, sheetrock, cement, steel, glass – raw materials – and uses these items to construct a house. The builder didn't create the cement, the two by fours or the glass. But he takes what's been made available to him and uses it to build the home.

Similarly, the enemy surveys us – our lifestyles, personalities, proclivities and tendencies - and he picks up the spiritual raw materials

---

[16] Rick Renner, *Sparkling Gems From The Greek*, 2003, pp.37-38.

that we've left lying around, the things we haven't dealt with. Maybe he sees some pride over here, notices a little rebellion there, takes some jealousy laying around in the front yard, uses a whole lot of insecurity that's laid up in the backyard, throws in some of that lust we've hidden in the garage . . . and voila! The devil has conspired with our flesh to construct strongholds in our lives. Christians are infamous for blowing the devil's rep way up. And yeah, he's public enemy number one, but we give him way too much credit. He's not a creator, he's just a builder. The problem is we keep giving him the raw materials to work with. It all starts with us.

Gotta Get Ya Mind Right

Notice the words Paul used in 2 Corinthians 10: 4-5 as he talked about strongholds – "arguments," "pretension," "thought." Paul's use of these words makes it clear the stronghold in our lives that must be demolished is in *the mind*. And it isn't just one thought that creates a stronghold. Strongholds are the result of thinking patterns. It's how we view life. It's our way of assessing situations. It's the audio loop that's playing in my head. It's the 3-D movie premiering in the theater of your mind. These thinking patterns are jacking us up, holding us back from accomplishing our God-given purpose, exuding vitality and leaving an indelible impact on the lives we touch. Yes, it's great that we're born-again, but you can love the Lord with all your heart and still be a prisoner to fear, insecurity, jealousy, anger, impatience, rejection issues and authority issues. So if we don't deal with the mental strongholds, we'll be saved but never experience the rich and satisfying John 10:10 life Jesus promised us. Getting our minds right is the essential first step in snatching our lives back.

Ever wonder why you keep repeating the same scenarios over and over and over in your life? Maybe not the exact same ones, but ever notice a variation on the same theme? It's usually because our thoughts around that situation or issue haven't been dealt with. Operation Snatch Back necessitates that we deal with our mental strongholds by doing the hard work of paying attention to what we're paying attention to.

Take Notes

I'd like to challenge you to start paying attention to what you're paying attention to. Begin by recording your predominant thoughts throughout each day for a week or so.[17] If you're anything like me or the dozens of people I've coached, your first instinct will be to try to steer your thoughts in a more positive direction before recording them. Nice try, but that's like trying to hold a beach ball underwater - eventually it pops up anyway. So let it rip! We need these thoughts recorded live and uncut, straight no chaser.

So if you spend five minutes visualizing your upcoming work presentation being a professional train wreck, jot those thoughts down. Repeatedly doubting if you have what it takes to finish that advanced degree? Write it down. Secretly a little jealous that your girlfriend's crushing her new job while you're still floundering career-wise? Take notes. Anxious over the upcoming family reunion where nosey Auntie Gladys is going to ask you for the one hundredth time why you aren't married/don't have kids/work so much? Yeah, you might need to journal about that one.

Once you've done that, take some time and peruse your list. Stunned by the negativity? Stupefied over the amount of self-deprecation?

---

[17] Section 3 of The Snatch Back Notebook has a page for this, or you can use the voice recorder on your smart phone.

Aghast at the bitterness or anger? Flabbergasted at the guilt? If your reaction to your list of thoughts is anything like mine, you can borrow my hand to pick your jaw off the floor and I'll hand you a box of Kleenex while we're at it. But paying attention to what you're paying attention to is like getting on the scale: the truth might be painful but at least you know what you're up against. But don't get discouraged - help and hope are on the way!

Once you have your handy little (or maybe not so little) list of thoughts, take some time to write down those things in your life with which you are most dissatisfied.[18] Unfulfilling job? Dead end romantic relationship? Toxic "friendships"? Perennially contentious family relationships? Financial crisis #496? You don't need to write a treatise – just a few words to describe each will do. The purpose here is to identify and capture the essence of each unsatisfactory situation.

Connect the Dots

As kids we've all done those connect the dot puzzles where you draw a line between the sequence of numbered dots until the outline of an object

---

[18] There's a spot right in Section 3 of The Snatch Back Notebook for this.

is revealed. Your next step will be to connect the dots between your thoughts and those less than satisfying areas of your life. While you may not see a picture, I'm almost sure you'll see a pattern. Really take the time to sit with your "what I'm most dissatisfied about" and "what I'm thinking about" lists side by side and I'll bet you'll draw lines connecting the majority of the items on the two lists.[19]

A while back when I first minded my mind, I knew my thoughts didn't exactly qualify me for Christian of The Year, but I had no idea how much damage they were doing to me spiritually, emotionally and psychologically. Once I really started paying attention to what I was thinking, I could immediately see a connection to my thoughts and my circumstances at the time. Almost every frustrating, disappointing situation in my life at the time was readily connected to a negative thought that I harbored. For instance, my dissatisfaction with the then-current state of my career was really due to my limiting belief that no one would pay to hear me speak and no one would buy a book that I wrote because no one knew I was alive. Sure, I kept telling myself that I was too busy with work

---

[19] Again, The Snatch Back Notebook will come in handy here.

and mommy duties to make time for it. Lies, all lies. *But a lie believed has more power than the truth rejected.* Yeah, I was busy, but not *that* busy. Thanks to the negative recorder loop full of lies playing my head, time and time again I talked myself out of it before I ever got started.

I say "recorder loop" because our thoughts are rarely random and isolated. If you took the time to pay attention to your thoughts even for a few days, I'm sure you noticed that certain thoughts reared their ugly heads repeatedly. Perhaps not the exact same thought but certainly variations on a theme. This recorder loop becomes the soundtrack for our lives, playing over and over again. Conflict with your spouse? Cue the music. Passed over for a promotion? Press play. Disagreement with your brother-in-law at a family gathering? Pump up the volume. We internalize that soundtrack, allowing it to affect our feelings. And once we get all up in our feelings? Lawd, help us! It takes nothing short of the power of the Holy Spirit to keep us from acting on them. These patterns of thinking represent mental and spiritual strongholds. From throwing shade to throwing punches, our negative behavior stems from our debilitating thoughts and the resulting emotions. And once we act on those feelings, we're sentenced to living with the results.

I had my client Kimberly mind her mind, paying attention to her thoughts and recording them for one week. And well, wouldn't you know it: Kimberly's negative self-talk was at the core of her defeatist perspective. She was constantly telling herself she wasn't "enough." After every meeting with a firm partner and every conference call with clients, the talk track in Kimberly's head reminded her "Well, that was good, but it wasn't perfect. *And you have to be perfect.*"

These thoughts were debilitating to Kimberly's self-esteem and, therefore, her career outlook. It was also affecting how Kimberly was being perceived by her firm's partners. Because she was frequently entertaining defeatist thoughts, Kimberly's enthusiasm would noticeably wane, causing her partners to doubt whether she really wanted a future at their firm. The thoughts inside Kimberly's head negatively affected how she was showing up to the outside world. Her thought life was ruining her purpose, destroying her vitality and dampening her impact. But identifying the root cause of the problem was only the beginning. We needed a strategy to deal with it.

Hand Me My Cutlass

During our first year of marriage, Lennon and I visited his birthplace, Jamaica. It was on this trip that hubby proudly announced he was going to purchase a cutlass. Now, I'm from New Orleans, the Lower Ninth Ward to be exact (read: the original 'hood). So when you say "cutlass" to me, I think "Oldsmobile Cutlass sittin' on 22s." But I soon learned that when Jamaicans say cutlass, they're referring to a machete-type apparatus. Who knew?

Upon arriving at the resort, Lennon promptly found a staff member to drive him to where cutlasses are sold in Jamaica, 'cause you may have guessed they don't sell those in the resort gift shop. Of course we couldn't bring it back into the U.S. sharpened, but once we were back home in Brooklyn Lennon knew exactly where to take the cutlass – the kind of thing that makes you wonder how well you really know a person. Regardless, we were now the proud owners of a sharpened cutlass.

One scholar of the Greek says that when Paul is telling us to take thoughts captive, the image is one of a Roman soldier who has taken an enemy soldier captive. And that Roman soldier has a sword in his hand and is constantly pushing the blade of that sword into the back of the enemy as he leads the enemy away into captivity.[20] The Roman soldier

would have to pay with his own life if he allowed that enemy captive to

escape. So any Roman soldier worth his salt was going to keep his eye and

sword trained on his captive, lest he pay the ultimate price. So if the

captive even looked like he was about to get out of hand, there goes a

limb! All because of the Roman soldier's sword.

As a believer, you have a sword - a cutlass to keep those enemy

thoughts in check, and you don't have to go all the way to Jamaica to get

one:

"Finally, be strong in the Lord and in his mighty power. Put on the full

armor of God, so that you can take your stand against the devil's schemes.

For our struggle is not against flesh and blood, but against the rulers,

against the authorities, against the powers of this dark world and against

the spiritual forces of evil in the heavenly realms. Therefore put on the full

armor of God, so that when the day of evil comes, you may be able to

stand your ground, and after you have done everything, to stand. Stand

firm then, with the belt of truth buckled around your waist, with the

---

[20] Renner, *Sparkling Gems in the Greek, Vol.1*, 2003, p. 77.

breastplate of righteousness in place, and with your feet fitted with the readiness that comes from the gospel of peace. In addition to all this, take up the shield of faith, with which you can extinguish all the flaming arrows of the evil one. Take the helmet of salvation and *the sword of the Spirit, which is the word of God*."[21]

As believers, the weapon we use to keep our minds in check is God's Word. But it's not enough to have a weapon. Like any law enforcement officer, you need to be *trained and ready* to use your weapon. Ever watch a movie scene where a person in danger gets their hands on a gun, but can't figure out how to put the clip in, can't take the safety off, and doesn't know how to aim? (Stereotypically a woman, so annoying!) I don't know about you, but I get so bothered just watching these debacles that I start rooting for the bad guy and screaming at the screen, "Just kill her already and get it over with!" Why? Because it's beyond frustrating to have a weapon at your disposal, but not know how to use it. You can be 6'2", 250 pounds of pure testosterone and be reduced to a spiritual damsel in distress when you don't know how to use what God has placed in your

---

[21] Ephesians 6:10-17, New International Version, emphasis mine.

spiritual arsenal. As believers, our greatest weapon against stinkin'

thinkin' is the Word of God.

So how do we use this weapon we have - the Word of God - to

take our enemy thoughts captive and make them obedient to Christ? In

other words, how do I use the Bible to snatch back my thoughts?

Cognitive behavioral therapy (CBT for short) is a form of psychotherapy

pioneered in the 1960's, the goal of which is to change the way people feel

by changing the patterns of thinking or the behaviors that are behind

people's difficulties. In other words, the goal of CBT is to change a

person's *feelings* by changing the way they *think*. But I didn't need a PhD.

in psychotherapy to know this. God's Word taught me:

"Don't copy the behavior and customs of this world, but *let God transform*

you into a new person by changing the way you think. Then you will learn

to know God's will for you, which is good and pleasing and

perfect."[22]When I change the pattern of my thinking, I change the pattern

of my actions. And changing the pattern of my actions will transform my

life. But it all starts in my mind. God transforms the lives of His children

---

[22] Romans 12:2, New Living Translation, emphasis mine.

by using His Word – the sword of the Spirit – to cut down belief systems and thought patterns that prevent us from living the lives of purpose, vitality and impact He has planned for us.

Do Your Work

Remember that list I had you make earlier in this chapter? The one where you connected the dots between areas of disappointment and frustration in your life and your limiting, negative beliefs? Yeah, that one. Well, pull it out because we're not done yet. If you're going to snatch your mind back from thoughts that are contrary to the life God has planned for you, you have to use your sword. Romans 12:2 teaches us that if you don't control what you think, you can't control what you do. So go through your list of limiting, negative beliefs and find one or two scriptures that apply to each situation and meditate daily on those scriptures.[23]

What Worked for Me?

I shared earlier that I procrastinated a good long while, avoiding writing this book because of the limiting belief that I just couldn't do it. And I constantly told myself that even if I did manage to write it, no one would

---

[23] You can use Section 3 of The Snatch Back Notebook to jot these down.

buy it for a laundry list of reasons that I could recite like the alphabet. But I finally got tired of not fully walking in my purpose, so I decided to write it – reasons be darned.

How'd I get there? By rehearsing God's Word to put the snatch on fear, doubt and discouragement, the root of which was lingering self-consciousness. I intentionally meditated on scriptures like 1 John 4:16, 18 which says in part, "We know how much God loves us, and we have put our trust in his love . . . Such love has no fear, because perfect love expels all fear."[24] I used God's Word to remind myself that my security isn't in my ability, looks, education or a title. I used God's Word to remind myself that my value comes from being created and loved by *Him*. I had to use God's Word to put the snatch on thoughts that were eroding my self-esteem. When I found myself making excuses for why I wasn't writing, I had to go back to God's Word for a freshly sharpened sword to battle that stuff. So I began to meditate on scriptures like Proverbs 3:6 and Psalm 18:29-31.

---

[24] New Living Translation

No matter what you're dealing with, there's a scripture to help align that thought with God's plan for your life. Jesus taught, "These words I speak, they are spirit & they are life." [25] There's power, life and freedom when you meditate on the Word of God - prayerfully pondering it throughout the day so when that negative thought tries to invade your mind, you reflect back to that scripture that speaks the truth about your situation. That's the kind of meditation on God's Word that enables us to take enemy thoughts captive. Sounds like Operation Snatch Back to me. Just sayin'.

Early and Often

Allowing defeating thoughts to run amuck in our minds unchecked is like a boulder rolling downhill – it picks up more speed and force with every inch of terrain it covers. The longer you let that negative thought run around, the stronger it becomes And then next thing you know, you want to be free from its grip on your mind and actions – but it's too strong. (That's why it's called a stronghold, not a weak hold.) When Paul talks about taking a thought captive, he uses a verb in the Greek that denotes the

---

[25] John 6:63

continuous action of a soldier taking an enemy captive. In other words, this isn't a one-time event. Just like it was the soldier's day to day job to keep an enemy soldier captive, it's our job daily to take and hold ungodly thoughts captive. We must take control of them early and often. It's got to be how we roll on the regular.

Many years ago, as a new mother, I was going through a challenging period. I was trying to juggle my very demanding job as a corporate attorney, fulfill wife and household roles, and still play a significant leadership role in our church's ministry. Putting in twelve to sixteen hour weekdays and full days at the church on Sundays left me mentally and physically exhausted.

Whether it was visions of Brooklynn becoming a mass murderer all because I couldn't show up at her preschool Christmas singalong or Lennon leaving me for someone ten years younger and twenty pounds lighter, every day I rehearsed disaster scenarios over and over in my mind. And every day I would drive to work boo-hooing, which was unusual for me because I don't cry easily or often. On day five of this pattern, I wondered to myself, "What in the world is wrong with you?" And then I felt God speak to my heart saying, "You're letting the devil punk you.

THE SNATCH BACK: RECLAIMING YOUR LIFE ONE TRUTH AT A TIME

That's what's wrong with you. Sure, you're stressed and things are chaotic. But the real problem is that you're entertaining all these negative, exaggerated and defeatist thoughts. You're not putting anything in check. You've been letting them run amuck in your mind for days now, and as a result the enemy is just straight up punking you." And it was then that I learned the spiritual discipline of *regularly* taking control of my thoughts early and often with the Word of God and the power of the Holy Spirit.

Perhaps that's what's happening to you. Maybe you're trying to put your thoughts in check, but not at the first sign of trouble. Maybe you're not immediately taking them captive and making them obedient to Christ. Or perhaps you're not aggressively making your thought life line up with the Word each day. And as a result the devil – the master builder that he is – conspires with your thought life and erects a stronghold in your spiritual walk. Boo, you gettin' punked. But you're not alone.

Remember my client Kimberly? She was getting punked, too. One of the keys to successfully addressing her thought patterns of inadequacy was *daily* meditating on scriptures that emphasized her worth in Christ. Not only did she meditate on these as a daily spiritual practice, we also worked to identify and anticipate the triggers that would cause these thoughts. After some reflection, Kimberly noticed that every month as she prepared client invoices, she'd begin to feel insecure about whether she'd logged enough billable hours to satisfy the partners and at the same time provided enough value to the client for the fees they were being charged. Even though she was consistently one of the highest billing associates and no client had ever pushed back on the hours she billed, Kimberly constantly worried about whether her performance was "perfect enough" to keep everyone happy. So in addition to her daily devotional, we developed a plan to step up her time in prayer, fasting and the Word about a week prior to her monthly invoicing duties. That way we got out in front of the negative pattern of thinking. This helped Kimberly put the snatch on those renegade thoughts *consistently, early and often.*

"Well Mo, that sounds like a lotta work." You think? Breaking news: you can't be lazy and be a Christian. Not a victorious one anyway. Sure, we need the power of the Holy Spirit to help us, but we've got to make the effort on our part. If you do, I'm sure you'll find it worth the energy. Kimberly certainly has.

Once she initiated Operation Snatch Back and got her thoughts aligned with God's Word, Kimberly's enthusiasm jumped noticeably, she became more innovative in solving her clients' legal problems, and partners and junior associates alike acknowledged the terrific team dynamic she was creating. I'm happy to report that she's on track to become a partner at her law firm - I fully expect to see Kimberly's name on the firm's letterhead within the next year. Most importantly, she's living her John 10:10 preferred life.

As Kimberly's story demonstrates, you've got to be persistent, proactive and aggressive with those negative thoughts. I mean, go straight prison yard on 'em. Remember: *in this life, you get what you fight for and you're gonna have whatever you settle for*. Don't settle for getting punked. Snatch your thoughts back!

Your Mind = Your Superpower

Lennon and our kids are all into superheroes. They binge-watch whole seasons of The Flash, Arrow, Super Girl, Legends of Tomorrow, Agents of Shield, Black Lightning, you name it. They've shown up to the box office for Justice League, Guardians of the Galaxy, Avengers: End Game, Wonder Woman and all the rest. I'm not really here for the superhero genre like that, but a couple years ago I was all up in the theater with the family for Black Panther.

If you didn't see the movie (because you apparently live under a rock), here's what Black Panther is all about: Hailing from the tiny fictional African nation of Wakanda, T'Challa (played by Chadwick Boseman) is suddenly thrust into the role of king when his father is assassinated. While to the outside world, it appears to be just another struggling nation on the African continent, Wakanda is actually one of the most technologically advanced nations in the world thanks to its abundant supply of the precious metal vibranium.

Vibranium's absorption of sound waves and other vibrations gives the metal its unusual strength. In fact The Black Panther's suit is made out of this precious metal. The radiation emanating from vibranium has permeated much of Wakanda's greenery, including the glowing, heart-shaped flower eaten by members of the Black Panther Tribe, giving superhuman abilities to whoever eats it. As the new leader, T'Challa must ultimately decide how to use the vibranium. He's faced with the monumental decision of leveraging vibranium for the good of mankind (but possibly exposing Wakanda to outsiders) or allowing Wakanda to continue to remain isolated, hoarding the precious metal.

Black Panther got me thinking about what kind of superpowers I'd like to have and how I'd use them for the good of mankind. You know, that whole "with great power comes great responsibility" thing. And while I'll never have teleportation abilities or superhuman strength (my personal faves), God has given me a mind to think and an imagination to dream. My thoughts can propel me into euphoria or sink me into despair. My mind can convince me all is well or all is lost. My imagination can be used to create scenarios of success or nightmares of failure.

Our thoughts influence our feelings, our feelings influence our actions, and our actions determine the outcomes with which we live. So our thoughts have a tremendous determinative effect on the lives we experience day in and day out. In short, *your mind is your superpower*. You can program it for success or failure depending on the thoughts you think, "for as a man thinketh in his heart, so is he.[26]" We become what we think.

And no, I don't believe in the oft-touted maxim "you can be anything you want to be." But as Tom Rath said "You cannot be anything

---

[26] Proverbs 23:7, King James Version

you want to be, but you can be a lot more of who you already are." A lot more of who God created you to be – with the purpose He gave you and the vitality and impact He wants you to have. Limiting thoughts hold many of us hostage to being a lot less than who we were created to be. For every superpower, there's a weakness. In the next three chapters, we're going to examine some mental kryptonite that will crush you every time if you don't take the proper precautions.

PART I

Reclaiming Your Thoughts

Chapter 4

Fear, Doubt and Worry

"**U**h, so that's it? You're done? *Like 'done done'?*" I asked incredulously. It pained me to even ask the question. "Yeah, 'Nique. I think this is it," she said.

I could hear her voice breaking, as she tried to hold back the tears. The resignation and defeat in her voice were so palpable I could reach out and touch them. Erica loved ministry and had wanted to be a pastor ever since I'd known her.

As young adults, we'd served in ministry together for several years, and I'd watched her grow as a believer and as a leader. At that time, I was what you might call a carnal Christian. Yeah, I loved Jesus and helped out in ministry, but I still liked to get my party on. Although I would later become a pastor, at that time in my life full-time ministry was nowhere on my agenda. Erica, on the other hand, was committed. She had become a believer as a teenager, and her walk had been consistent since that time. The call on Erica's life to be a pastor was confirmed time and time again by her local church leaders and members alike. Stevie Wonder could see it.

Eventually, I headed to law school while Erica headed to seminary, each of us relocating to pursue the next chapter of our lives. A bright and eager student, Erica devoured the challenging reading and writing assignments her professors threw at her, excelled in her internships and graduated with distinction. Having her sights set on becoming a local church pastor, Erica prayed, fasted, applied for numerous positions at all levels, and busied herself serving at her local church. Then she waited for the offers to roll in. They never did.

"What do you do when you've done all the right things, checked all the boxes and still no answer?" Erica asked me. "You just stand," I replied, quoting the lyrics from a gospel song that was popular at the time. But at the time those words sounded so hollow and inadequate, even to me as I spoke them. "I'm just afraid this will never happen and I will have wasted all my time, not to mention all the money I borrowed for school. Maybe me becoming a pastor was just a pipe dream. Maybe I never really heard from God in the first place," Erica tearfully confided.

Fear and doubt. Yeah, they're close relatives, like first cousins or something. We all know them because we've all felt them. We've all felt them because they're a natural part of human existence. When we talk about living a life of purpose, vitality and impact, fear and doubt are public enemy numbers one and two. They're on America's most wanted list for highjacking dreams, stealing confidence and murdering futures. They usually roll together. And the comorbidity of fear and doubt usually creates worry.

When we worry we waste valuable energy rehearsing what could go wrong, detracting energy from finding a viable solution. When we worry, we bow down to the fear that the future will live up to our exceedingly low expectations. When we worry, we idolize difficulty not yet realized. When you think about it, worrying is simply worshipping the problem.

Each of fear, doubt and worry is an enemy to our souls. Together, this spiritual triumvirate assaults our minds, oppresses our wills and dictates our emotions. Never is the work of these dictators so evident as when we're desperately waiting on God to show up in our circumstances. Whether it's professional like in Erica's case, financial, and relational or otherwise, it seems as if standing on a promise from God is a magnet for fear, doubt and worry.

Promises, Promises

Ever receive a promise from God? Maybe your promise came in the form of a scripture that really resonated in your heart. Perhaps it came via a prophetic word you received from a trusted spiritual leader. Or maybe you sensed God speaking a promise to you during your prayer time. However it comes, everyone gets excited, euphoric even, when they believe they've received a promise from God.

Sometimes the promised event, miracle or circumstance comes to pass quickly. But more often than not, there's a gap in between the time we receive the promise and the point in time when we experience what was promised. While we're waiting, God uses these divine delays to shape our characters, purify our hearts and test our motives.

And the wait in between can be just as painful as the initial promise is exciting. That in between time is what I call the "messy meantime." God tells you you're going to have a successful business. But He doesn't tell you that you're going to try three different business models that fail, and when you do find the one that works it's going to take seven years before that business is self-sustaining, let alone profitable. And you will wonder if you're going to starve to death in the meantime. God promises you'll recover physically, but what He doesn't say is you'll need multiple surgeries, numerous medications and physical rehabilitation in the meantime. And the longer the meantime, the more doubt and its twin fear, and its cousin worry begin to creep in. Sometimes that meantime is so painful, it can make you go from being excited about what God has promised you to wondering if God is even real. And we roll our eyes heavenward, thinking, "Promises, promises."

Strategically, there's never a better time for the enemy of our souls to start running mind games on us than when we're on the verge of living in our purpose on purpose. The thief who wants to steal your joy, kill your purpose and destroy your future whispers in your ear, "Did God *really* promise that? And if He did, did he really promise that to *you*? Yeah, he may have promised you that, but that was *before* you did [fill in the blank with your latest sin]. Chile, ain't no way He'll bless you after that."

When the enemy begins to attack our minds with an onslaught of fear, doubt and worry, we need to remind ourselves of God's faithfulness and encourage ourselves with lessons from spiritual giants both past and present.

#Goals

I can't think of anyone in the Bible who had to wait longer than Abraham. And I can't think of a better example of *how* to wait than Abraham.

Abraham was an idol worshipper who was hand-picked by God to start the Jewish nation and begin the lineage of Jesus Christ. We first meet him in Genesis 11, where Abraham is introduced as the son of Terah, who was an idol worshipper himself. And in Genesis 12, God first promises to bless Abraham:

> "The LORD had said to Abram, "Leave your native country, your relatives, and your father's family, and go to the land that I will show you. I will make you into a great nation. I will bless you and make you famous, and you will be a blessing to others. I will bless those who bless you and curse those who treat you with contempt. All the families on earth will be blessed through you." So Abram

departed as the LORD had instructed, and Lot went with him. *Abram was seventy-five years old when he left Haran.*"[27]

When we pick up the story in Genesis 21, here's what's happening:

"The LORD kept his word and did for Sarah exactly what he had promised. She became pregnant, and she gave birth to a son for Abraham in his old age. This happened at just the time God had said it would. And Abraham named their son Isaac. Eight days after Isaac was born, Abraham circumcised him as God had commanded. *Abraham was 100 years old when Isaac was born.*"[28]

So in Genesis 12 we have Abraham receiving the promise of a son when he is 75 years old and in Genesis 21 we have Sarah actually giving birth to Isaac when Abraham is 100 years old. I'm no math wiz, but that's a long time. Twenty-five years long to be exact. And during those twenty-five years Abraham, the patriarch of the Jewish race and the father of the Christian faith, endured a very painful wait. Here's the highlight reel from Abraham's messy meantime:

---

[27] Genesis 12:1-4 New Living Translation, emphasis mine.
[28] Genesis 21:1-5, New Living Translation

God tells Abraham to leave his father's family, including his nephew Lot, and go to Canaan, but Abraham takes Lot with him anyway.[29]

Abraham has to relocate to Egypt in order to escape a famine in Canaan; while Abraham accumulates a great deal of wealth while he's living in Egypt, some commentators believe that he has no altar, no worship and is essentially cut off from communication with God.[30]

When Abraham and his wife Sarah arrive in Egypt, Abraham is fearful that, because Sarah was so beautiful, the Egyptian pharaoh will kill him so the king can take Sarah as his wife. So Abraham lies and says that Sarah is his sister. The Egyptian pharaoh takes Sarah into his court to be one of his wives, only to find mysterious plagues breaking out against him and his household. The pharaoh puts two and two together, correctly concluding this is all

---

[29] Genesis 12:1
[30] Genesis 12:6-9

happening because Sarah is actually married to Abraham.

Abraham and Sarah are unceremoniously dismissed from Egypt.[31]

Once the famine is over, Abraham who has become very wealthy, goes back to Canaan. His herdsmen & Lot's herdsmen end up in conflict over grazing and water rights, so Abraham and Lot go their separate ways.[32]

Lot ends up living near Sodom and Gomorrah; he gets caught up in a war between some of the Kings, and Abraham has to rescue Lot by going to war with some of these kings.[33] Presumably, Abraham would have been spared this conflict if he'd obeyed God and never taken Lot with him when he left Haran.

Abraham and Sarah get tired of waiting on God for a son and decide they would help Him out by having Abraham father a child

---

[31] Genesis 12:10-20
[32] Genesis 13:5-13
[33] Genesis 14:1-16

with Sarah's servant. As a result, Ishmael is born, resulting in centuries of conflict in the Middle East that still exists today.[34] Abraham goes to live in Gerar. He arrives there and is again afraid the king will want to kill him and marry Sarah, so Abraham lies again saying Sarah is his sister. And we have a repeat of what happened with the Egyptians. [35]

Whew, Chile! Abraham's meantime was good and messy! But even through all that, he's still called the father of faith and is used in Hebrews 6 as *the* example to imitate for obtaining God's promises. When it comes to faith in God, Abraham is officially #goals. So what does the Bible tell us Abraham did right? Here's what I believe was key to Abraham coming out like a champ in the end:

"Even when there was no reason for hope, Abraham kept hoping - believing that he would become the father of many nations. For God had said to him, "That's how many descendants you will have!" And Abraham's faith did not weaken, even though, at about

---

[34] Genesis 16
[35] Genesis 20:1-18

100 years of age, he figured his body was as good as dead—and so was Sarah's womb. *Abraham never wavered in believing God's promise. In fact, his faith grew stronger, and in this he brought glory to God. He was* <u>*fully convinced*</u> *that God is able to do whatever he promises. And because of Abraham's faith, God counted him as righteous.*"[36]

This is an extremely powerful passage of scripture, and it's rendered even more powerfully in The Message Bible. A contemporary idiomatic translation of the original Biblical languages Hebrew and Greek, The Message Bible gives shades of meaning and color to the scriptures. And this is how The Message Bible renders Romans 4:18-22:

"Abraham didn't focus on his own impotence and say, "It's hopeless This hundred-year-old body could never father a child." Nor did he survey Sarah's decades of infertility and give up. He didn't tiptoe around God's promise asking cautiously skeptical questions. *He plunged into the promise and came up strong, ready*

---

[36] Romans 4:18-22, New Living Translation, emphasis mine

for God, sure that God would make good on what he had said. That's why it is said, 'Abraham was declared fit before God by trusting God to set him right.'" [37]

I'm sure during that twenty-five year period of waiting on God, Abraham battled more than his fair share of fear, doubt and worry. With no Bible verses, Christian podcasts or prayer partners to hold him up, Abraham plunged himself into the promise God had given him. Abraham saturated his mind and heart with what God said about his situation.

What does plunging ourselves in the promises of God look like in practice? Andrew Murray, the South African theologian and evangelist, described it as *"holding the Word of God in the mind until it has affected every area of one's life and character."*[38] Plunging ourselves into God's Word means to ponder over it, contemplate it, repeat it, review it, and meditate on it. Plunging ourselves into the promises of God means consistently filling our minds with thoughts of His promises.

---

[37] Romans 4:19-25, The Message Bible, emphasis mine.
[38] Ron Rhodes, *1001 Unforgettable Quotes About God, Faith, and the Bible*, p. 20.

Chow Time

Abraham meditated on God's promise to him until it shaped how he saw his circumstances. One definition of meditation used in the Bible is similar to a cow chewing cud. First, the cow gulps the food down, then regurgitates it back up out of the stomach into its mouth and chews on it again. The cow does this several times, so that when the food finally remains in the stomach, it's easily digested and therefore, the vitamins and nutrients in the food can then be absorbed into the bloodstream, giving the cow physical energy and strength.

This image reminds me of the Bible verse, *"When your words came, I ate them;* they were my joy and my heart's delight."[39] Abraham ate – meditated on again and again - God's promise for his life until every area of his heart and mind were affected by that promise. This means that whenever the enemy came with a worrisome thought designed to steal Abraham's peace, God's promise was dwelling in his mind so fully that Abraham was able to overpower that worry with what God had said. The result of plunging himself into God's promise was that Abraham became

---

[39]Jeremiah 15:16 New International Version, emphasis mine

fully convinced that God would do exactly what He said, and therefore Abraham was able to keep believing until the promise came to pass. God's promises are a good home-cooked meal to feast on when our souls become famished from waiting.

When our son Judah was a toddler and I was trying to get him to eat, I'd have him flex his bicep. I would tell Judah, "Mama's doing a 'muscle check.'" If Judah flexed his bicep and it didn't "feel strong enough", didn't "feel big enough," then he had to eat some more. We need to do a spiritual muscle check. And when we do, we may find that we don't have enough Word *in* us for the fight that's coming *against* us. We don't have enough Word in us to hold us down when the winds of doubt begin to blow and the waves of fear roll through our lives. All because we're not "eating" God's Word.

Perhaps you've received a promise from God, but because of adversity, personal failure or simply the passage of time, you've allowed fear and doubt to rob your life of purpose, vitality and impact. Maybe you're struggling to keep believing "in the meantime." Or perhaps you're feeling trapped in your messy meantime, worrying if you really heard from God in the first place. We can see from Abraham's highlight reel that

102

he didn't achieve this level of saturation in God's promises overnight, and neither will we.

One of the things I really love about the Bible is it's transparency in showing the very human side of our heroes of the faith. The writer of Abraham's story doesn't cover up the fact that, after waiting ten years for their promised son, Abraham and Sarah hatched their own cock-eyed plan to achieve what God had yet to deliver on by having Abraham impregnate a surrogate. Yeah, Abraham and Sarah got ahead of God, and Ishmael was the result. But without this mistake, we'd be deprived of a valuable lesson: *"that God's grace is greater than man's sin and can accomplish God's best even when men do their worst.*[40]"

If you've allowed fear, doubt or worry to stall, steal or destroy your life purpose, Abraham's story is a wonderfully encouraging example of how to not allow your dirt-road detour become your permanent highway path. Admit it to yourself, confess it to God, and renew your commitment to daily thinking, decision-making and acting in faith.[41] And

---

[40] Warren W. Wiersbe, *The Warren Wiersbe Bible Commentary, The Complete Old Testament in One Volume*, p. 72.
[41] You can journal your thoughts about this in Section 4 of The Snatch Back Notebook.

the starting point for renewing those commitments is plunging yourself in God's Word.

It took Abraham a while to get it but, despite his failures and shortcomings, he never stopped eating God's promise, and it sustained him until he was ultimately holding baby Isaac in his arms. In fact, Abraham was so convinced of God's promise to make him the father of many nations that when God requested that Abraham sacrifice Isaac on Mount Moriah, Abraham prepared to do so without question or hesitation.[42] Abraham apparently believed that even if Isaac was sacrificed, God would somehow still make good on His promise.

New Faith, Who Dis?

But how do we reconcile the Abraham who lied about his wife to save his own behind with the Abraham who was ready to sacrifice his son Isaac, on whom he had waited twenty-five years? I've read these passages and wondered, "Is this even the same dude?" 'Cause Abraham is up on Mount Moriah looking brand, brand new!

---

[42] Genesis 22:1-12

The answer is *Abraham's faith grew in time over time*. And so can ours. Our faith isn't a static, unchanging barometer of our relationship with God. Rather, our faith is dynamic with an incredible capacity to grow and expand as we build our relationship with God over time. Through all his messy meantime misadventures, God and Abraham developed a real relationship through the processes of mistakes, confession, forgiveness and restoration. And our messy meantime can produce the same level of closeness, trust and dependency on the Lord if we continue to faithfully eat God's Word despite our bouts with fear, doubt and worry.

It's time to get your grub on, and the Word of God is a full seven-course spiritual meal. Meditating on God's Word is a spiritual discipline that takes time and intention, but yields so much benefit. Head over to the Section 4 of The Snatch Back Notebook for an outline of how to begin the practice of meditating on God's promises.

That Bounce Back

As kids, many of us had those freestanding punching bags. The fun of playing with those was that no matter how hard you drop kicked that sucker, it would bounce right back into its upright position. The bag might bend backwards or sideways, but it wouldn't fall down. The reason the bag didn't fall down even when hit with a powerful force is because it was weighted on the bottom by something heavier than it, by something stronger than the force that hit it. It's base was secure.

Snatching our minds back from fear, doubt and worry requires us to be spiritually weighted by a secure base - something heavier than the negative thoughts assaulting our minds. God's Word is that secure base.

The Word of God will hold you down while you're waiting for the promise to come to pass. And the reason you won't fall over is because God's promise in His Word is stronger and more potent than whatever tries to dropkick you. Real faith doesn't mean that you won't get hit with fear, doubt or worry - it just means that you have supernatural God-given ability to rebound from the hit and not fall apart. Plunging ourselves into God's promises in His Word is how we spiritually get weighted on the bottom and reclaim our thoughts from fear, doubt and worry. It's how you get your bounce back. Take Operation Snatch Back to the next level by diving into and eating up God's Word.

Delayed But Not Denied

My friend Erica and I lost touch over the years, but when we finally reconnected the joy in her voice was such a welcome contrast to our last conversation. She candidly shared how much she'd wrestled with fear and doubt over the years. At one point, Erica got so tired of waiting for a job in ministry she even went back to her old career in accounting, which she hated with a passion. But eventually, twelve years after graduating from seminary, a ministry door had opened. Erica was having the time of her life serving as the lead pastor of a thriving local church right outside Atlanta, Georgia. She was living her preferred John 10:10 life.

When Erica reflected on how those twelve years of waiting impacted her, she said "You know 'Nique, I knew the Bible, but I didn't 'know, know' it. Yeah, I had verses memorized and I knew the Greek and the Hebrew. And I studied the Bible everyday so I could put together great sermons, and I even had daily devotion. But I wasn't reading the Bible *intentionally*. I didn't have the daily discipline of *intentionally* fortifying my soul and spirit with God's promises about my purpose and calling. After about five years of waiting, I knew I had to do something different or I wasn't going to make it. So I started meditating on God's promises to feed my faith and starve my doubts to death. Everyday I would tell myself, 'E, it's just matter of time before what God spoke to you in the night is manifested in the light.'"

Whether you've been waiting twelve years or twelve days, don't let the triumvirate of fear, doubt and worry hijack your purpose, steal your impact and kill your vitality. Plunge yourself into God's Word and come up strong so you can execute Operation Snatch Back. What God spoke to your heart in the night will eventually manifest in the light.

In our next chapter, we'll take a hard look at another area of our thought life that prevents us from living the John 10:10 life Jesus promised us – the trap of other people's opinions.

Chapter 5

Other People's Opinions

There's a well-known fable that goes like this:

"A Man and his son were once going with their Donkey to market. As they were walking along by its side a countryman passed them and said: "You fools, what is a Donkey for but to ride upon?"

So the Man put the Boy on the Donkey and they went on their way. But soon they passed a group of men, one of whom said: "See that lazy youngster, he lets his father walk while he rides."

So the Man ordered his Boy to get off, and got on himself. But they hadn't gone far when they passed two women, one of whom said to the other: "Shame on that lazy lout to let his poor little son trudge along."

Well, the Man didn't know what to do, but at last he took his Boy up before him on the Donkey. By this time they had come to the town, and the passers-by began to jecr and point at them. The Man stopped and asked what they were scoffing at. The men said: "Aren't you ashamed of yourself for overloading that poor Donkey of yours—you and your hulking son?"

The Man and Boy got off and tried to think what to do. They thought and they thought, till at last they cut down a pole, tied the Donkey's feet to it, and raised the pole and the Donkey to their shoulders. They went along amid the laughter of all who met them till they came to Market Bridge, when the Donkey, getting one of his feet loose, kicked out and caused the Boy to drop his end of the pole. In the struggle the Donkey fell over the bridge, and his fore-feet being tied together he was drowned.

"That will teach you," said an old man who had followed them: "Please all, and you will please none."[43]

This fable is a humorous illustration of a quote often attributed to John Lydgate, the English monk and poet, "You can please some of the people all of the time, you can please all of the people some of the time, but you can't please all of the people all of the time." Looks like the man, his son and the donkey each found this out real quick! But does this mean we should ignore what others have to say about our personal choices?

---

[43] Aesop, *The Man, The Boy and The Donkey. In The Harvard Classics, Aesop's Fables*, pp.1909–14.

111

As believers, we're called to exist in community and live a life that will cause others to be drawn to the God we serve. Several scriptures admonish us as believers to be careful in our conduct because others are watching, including:

"Be careful to live properly among your unbelieving neighbors. Then even if they accuse you of doing wrong, they will see your honorable behavior, and they will give honor to God when he judges the world." 1 Peter 2:12[44]

"Live wisely among those who are not believers, and make the most of every opportunity. Let your conversation be gracious and attractive so that you will have the right response for everyone." Colossians 4:5-6[45]

So we can see from these scriptures that God thinks other people's opinions of us certainly matter. Therefore, it's incumbent upon us to care about both our reputation (who people think we are) as well as our

---

[44] New Living Translation
[45] New Living Translation

character (who we are when no one's looking). We're also encouraged as believers to seek wise counsel or advice, which is another kind of opinion:

"Plans go wrong for lack of advice; many advisers bring success." Proverbs 15:22[46]

"Get all the advice and instruction you can, so you will be wise the rest of your life." Proverbs 19:20[47]

So no doubt God wants us to care about what others think of us and value others' opinions. In fact, He actually designed us humans to give a hoot. Maslow's hierarchy of needs is a theory first espoused in 1943 by American psychologist Abraham Maslow which describes the needs that motivate human behavior. According to Maslow's hierarchy, all human beings have certain basic physiological and physical needs, such as food, water, shelter and safety.

But once those basic needs are sufficiently satisfied, humans then focus on having their needs for belonging, love and esteem fulfilled. In other words, acceptance by others is second only to three hot's and a cot.

---

[46] New Living Translation
[47] New Living Translation

This basic human need for belonging drives us relationally in every way, from living in communities to getting married and starting families. And it also causes us to value the opinions of others. If we want to live with others and feel that sense of belonging, we must consider how our actions will impact them. We have to value their opinions, at least to some degree. We must give some kind of a hoot. Therefore, the need to belong and be accepted acts as a subconscious deterrent to antisocial behavior for most individuals. By first grade we all learn that the kid who picks his nose at the lunch table won't have any friends. Learning this is a good thing. And we learn that if we go around being zero percent nice to people on the regular we'll end up with zero friends. Another good lesson to learn.

But there's a point at which our need for acceptance can be unhealthy. Yes, there's wisdom and safety in a multitude of counselors, but there's no substitute for knowing what the Wise Counselor, Jesus, has spoken to our hearts. And if we're not careful, we can allow our thoughts to be inordinately shaped by what other people think. And when other people's opinions get all up in our heads, it's only a matter of time before we start basing our actions on what they will think. I gotta confess: at times I've felt like the man and the boy, but more often than not, I've been the donkey in Aesop's fable. There have been times in my life when I've denied myself permission to take a particular course of action because I allowed other people's dissenting opinions to drown out what I knew was right for me. And each time, I've regretted it.

While I never loved practicing law, at one point in my career I actually had a role I could tolerate on most days and even enjoy on some others. I thought I was performing pretty well, and apparently my leadership thought so too because I was offered a big promotion. The new role had all of the bells and whistles that screamed high potential, upwardly mobile boss – an impressive title, more direct reports, more visibility and a bigger salary.

The only catch was this new role was even less interesting to me than my current one, and would demand even more hours and additional travel. But there was a lot of pressure from the top to take it. And I had already declined a previous promotion because it would have required my family to relocate. This one was local, and this type of role didn't come around often. I prayed and turned the decision over again and again in my mind: Should I take it? What would be the ramifications if I didn't?

Would declining the opportunity signal that I wasn't serious about my career? Would my boss, who was also a very valuable sponsor, stop supporting me? What would my colleagues think?

As part of my due diligence, I had conversations with key people within the company that I respected. Of course, they all said some version of "This is a wonderful opportunity! You'll be great in this role! Go for it!" Although my gut kept telling me no, I finally accepted the position. Do I even need to tell you the rest of the story?

While I did well in the role, I was even more miserable than before. I hated everything about it – the work, the hours, my new boss, my new clients, you name it. I would drive to work in the morning with knots in my stomach and then put on my game face as soon as I hit the parking lot of the corporate offices. I endured migraine headaches for months on end and rarely got a good night's sleep. I was physically and mentally drained. What had I done? I had succumbed to the pressure of other people's expectations for me rather than remain true to my own inclinations.

When we allow other people's opinions to override what we know God has whispered in our ear, we allow the enemy of our souls to rob us.

And then we have the nerve to wonder why we're lacking purpose, vitality and impact. When we allow the opinions of others to unduly influence our thoughts, feelings, and ultimately our actions, we've set out like the man, the boy and the donkey on a path to pleasing no one, especially our Creator. And when we allow ourselves to be moved away from pleasing God, there's no way we can expect to live our preferred John 10:10 life.

Thanks to being human, none of us is going to be perfectly pleasing to God this side of heaven, but that doesn't mean we can't take a few notes from The Best To Ever Do It.

The G.O.A.T.

Jesus was an incredible teacher, healer, listener and friend who came onto the scene when the Jews were under Roman rule. Due to disagreement on how to deal with Roman oppression, several Jewish factions arose: Pharisees (isolationists who adhered to Jewish ceremonial laws with anesthetizing conformity), Sadducees (assimilationist aristocrats who thought cozying up to the Romans was the right move), Zealots (militarists who favored armed resistance to Roman rule) and Essenes (who formed monastery-like communities and prayed for the Messiah to come). Each of these groups expected The Messiah to take up their cause.

117

Jesus' unwillingness to adopt their agenda put him in constant conflict with these groups, especially the Pharisees and Sadducees. Much to the chagrin of these various factions, Jesus completely shunned identity boundaries. As a result, His ministry was hugely popular with the impoverished and disenfranchised Jewish and non-Jewish masses alike. What the Pharisees and the other groups failed to realize was that Jesus had an assignment from His Heavenly Father way before any of them had an opinion.[48]

But being hated on by a group of weird strangers is one thing. Having *your people* curve you is a whole 'nother thing. When Jesus returned to His hometown, Matthew 13:53-58 says "he gave a lecture in the meetinghouse. He made a real hit, impressing everyone. 'We had no idea he was this good!' they said. 'How did he get so wise, get such ability?' *But in the next breath they were cutting him down:* 'We've known him since he was a kid; he's the carpenter's son. We know his mother, Mary. We know his brothers James and Joseph, Simon and Judas. All his sisters live here. *Who does he think he is?*' They got their noses all

---

[48] Check out Revelation 13:8

out of joint. But Jesus said, 'A prophet is taken for granted in his hometown and his family.' He didn't do many miracles there because of their hostile indifference.[49]"

This wasn't exactly the welcome home party one might expect for The Son of God. Just like the religious factions of His day, the hometown crowd in Nazareth had an opinion about Jesus and His ministry. And it wasn't positive. They couldn't knock the anointing and power with which He ministered, so they tried to invalidate His authority by making Him seem too common and ordinary to merit respect and attention. *When people can't invalidate what you've accomplished, they'll try to minimize who you are.* "Who does He think he is?" That question was laced with the cyanide of their negative opinions. The insinuation was that Jesus was getting a lil too big for His britches. In a New York minute, the hometown crowd went from being wowed by Jesus' teaching to accusing Him of thinking more highly of Himself than His earthly pedigree warranted. They went from admiring His teaching and oratory ability in one breath to "cutting him down in the next breath." Sound familiar?

---

[49] Matthew 13:53-58, The Message Bible, emphasis mine.

Not only are other people's opinions often in conflict with what we know we need to do, they are also notoriously shifty. But *you can't stay on the merry-go round of other people's views and wonder why you're dizzy.* Other people's opinions may be informative and interesting, but they are by no means determinative or dispositive. Remember: the right to an opinion does not make the opinion right.

If being hated on by Jewish factions and the hometown crowd weren't enough, Jesus also had to deal with being dissed by His own family. Two cases in point:

"Jesus went back home, and once again such a large crowd gathered that there was no chance even to eat. When Jesus' *family* heard what he was doing, they *thought he was crazy* and went to get him under control." Mark 3:20-21[50]

"and Jesus' brothers said to him, "Leave here and go to Judea, where your followers can see your miracles! You can't become famous if you hide like this! *If you can do such wonderful things,*

---

[50] Contemporary English Version

show yourself to the world!" For even his brothers didn't believe

in him." John 7:3-5 [51]

Did you read that? The people closest to Jesus – His own family - thought He was out of His mind and doubted Him. That's next-level messed up.

Ouch! That Hurts!

Talk about being the subject of dissenting opinions. Facing disapproval, disdain and eventually hatred, Jesus somehow managed to stay true to who He was and His mission on earth. We often think of Jesus as this superhero who roamed the earth leaping over physical and emotional obstacles in a single bound (after all, He did walk on water). But Jesus wasn't impervious to emotional hurt and pain. The Bible says Jesus experienced all the same emotions we do, yet He never sinned.[52] So no doubt Jesus felt more than a tad chilly with all that shade being thrown at Him. I'm sure His feelings were hurt. I'm sure He felt ridiculed and betrayed. And yet He didn't let those emotions dictate His moves.

---

[51] New Living Translation
[52] Check out Hebrews 4:15.

Can you imagine what would have happened if Jesus had allowed the opinions of others to drown out that still small voice inside Him? What would have happened if Jesus allowed the opinions of others to cause Him to shrink back from the purpose and calling God had ordained for Him since before the foundation of the world? Well, for starters, all the many miracles we read about in the Gospels never would have occurred – no blind eyes opened, no deaf ears hearing again, no dead daughters raised to life, no lepers healed, no withered hands restored, just to name a few. And you and I would have absolutely no chance of ever living our John 10:10 life. So where in the world did Jesus get the courage to rise above others' opinions and live as who God called Him to be?

What Daddy Said

When Jesus declared to the Pharisees in John 8:14 that He was the light of the world, Jesus was establishing His unique divine identity and purpose, claiming that He is the exclusive source of spiritual light for mankind. True to form, the Pharisees, who didn't believe in His divinity, called him a liar. Most of us would set it off if somebody called us a liar. But not Jesus, whose level of calm was on one thousand. He simply replied, "*I know* where I came from and where I am going. *But you don't know* where

I am from or where I am going."[53] Jesus was so uber-confident in who He was that neither mounting disbelief nor open hostility to Him and His ministry couldn't shake him.

The key to snatching back your mind from other people's opinions is being so firmly persuaded in your own God-reinforced opinion that theirs simply lack the power to sway you. Jesus arose early every morning and went to a quiet spot, away from the crowds and His disciples, to spend time with God. In this time, Jesus undoubtedly received instruction and direction for His day. But I believe Jesus also received something so much more than a divine to-do list. Jesus received affirmation from His Heavenly Father. I believe in those times of quiet devotion, God continued the affirming work He publicly began at the beginning of Jesus' ministry:

"The moment Jesus came up out of the baptismal waters, the skies opened up and he saw God's Spirit—it looked like a dove— descending and landing on him. And along with the Spirit, a voice: *'This is my Son, chosen and marked by my love, delight of my life.'*" Matthew 3:16-17[54]

---

[53] John 8:14, Contemporary English Version, emphasis mine
[54] The Message Bible

In speaking those words, God showed His approval of Jesus' obedience in being baptized. But much more importantly, God also expressed His affirmation of who Jesus was to Him and how God felt about Him – Jesus was God's son, whom God loved and in whom God delighted. Jesus was the apple of God's eye. And Jesus hadn't even done a single miracle yet. Let that sink in. It wasn't about anything Jesus did *for* God, it was about who He was *to* God.

Daily time with the Father gave Jesus a fresh opportunity to be saturated in God's affirmation, and that level of love and acceptance brought about a supreme confidence. A kind of confidence that allows the one receiving it to hold God's opinion in higher esteem than any other.

I know it's corny, but when my kids were little I had them repeat certain affirmations frequently as a way of reminding them of who they were and what they were capable of. When our son Judah was about eight years old, a boy in his class used a racial slur against him. When Judah came home and told me about it, he was quite calm and impressively matter-of-fact about the incident. Of course, Lennon and I addressed the issue with his teacher and the other student.

Once the dust settled, I asked Judah why he wasn't more upset about the incident. "Mama, if someone is that ignorant their opinion doesn't even factor into my consciousness," Judah said. "And besides Mama, you always tell me I'm your highly intelligent boy capable of doing all things through Christ, and I believe what you say over what anybody else says. Now, I'm glad we went to school and handled it, but I'm good." When faced with an insulting, racist slur, Judah chose to believe what his parents said about him rather than believe someone else's ignorant opinion. Looks like reciting those affirmations wasn't so corny after all.

Jesus chose to believe what His Father said about Him over what anybody else had to say. Jesus knew He was the Son of God called to be the Messiah, the Savior of the world. Being doubted by religious factions, neighbors or even His family couldn't shake Jesus from His identity and His assignment. Like Judah, their uninformed, limited and erroneous opinions didn't factor into Jesus' consciousness.

In my own life, I've often found a direct correlation between the amount of time I spend with God focusing on His plans for me and my ability to resist living under the tyranny of people's opinions. The more

THE SNATCH BACK: RECLAIMING YOUR LIFE ONE TRUTH AT A TIME

time I spend with Him, the more I can give other people's opinions the Heisman.

Do Your Work

What about you? Have you at times allowed the opinions of others to override what you know God is speaking to your heart? Where in your life do you need to snatch back your thoughts from being drowned out by other people's views?

Make a commitment today to spend daily time listening to God through reading the Bible, prayer and worship. When you do this, He'll instruct, guide and affirm you. Check out Section 5 of The Snatch Back Notebook for some practical guidance on how to do this.

Now, let's look at the final area of our thought life that the enemy of our souls uses to steal our purpose, kill our impact and destroy our vitality – self-doubt.

Chapter 6

Self-Doubt

She just sat there, staring at the blank piece of paper. I thought perhaps she didn't understand the instructions I had just given, so I repeated them, this time in a slightly louder voice. "And if you have any questions, just raise your hand and I'll come over to you," I said looking in her direction. I was a workshop presenter at a women's ministry conference. I had been asked to teach on fulfilling our God-given potential and, since one of my gifts is to help others blow the roof off their limitations, I was ecstatic.

As part of my workshop, I had the ladies do several exercises, one of which was to do a self-inventory of their natural talents and abilities. As the other participants eagerly dove into this exercise, this woman kept staring at the paper, writing nothing. Sensing she was stuck, I made my way over to give her some assistance. As I approached her to offer my help, I saw tears welling up in her eyes. "Is something wrong?" I asked, pulling up a chair next to her. "Uh, no . . . not really. Um, it's just that, well, you know, uh . . . I'm not good at anything." "Nothing?" I asked incredulously. "Nothing," she said in a pained whisper.

Some of us know what it's like to struggle with low self-esteem and an overall lack of confidence. If asked to list our faults, we could sit for hours rattling off all our issues. But when someone asks us to list some positive, healthy things about ourselves, we come up empty. Some of us find it hard to receive a sincere compliment, let alone give ourselves one. For years I struggled with being self-conscious. If someone admired something I was wearing, I felt compelled to downplay it with comments like, "What? This ole thing? Girl, I've had it for years." I had a hard time accepting a simple compliment, and an even harder time acknowledging what my strengths were. And as a result, I couldn't get out of my own way, embrace who God made me to be and develop my gifts. Whenever we allow this to happen, we think, act and live small, allowing the enemy to steal our impact. When we're mired in self-doubt and insecurity, we don't need anybody else to handicap our potential. Insecurity is a tool the enemy of our souls uses to get us to kneecap ourselves. And it hurts like heck.

But despite how we see ourselves, we all have gifts, strengths and abilities that God wants used for His glory. And I'm not just giving some feel-good pep talk here. 1 Peter 4:10 says "Each of you has been blessed with one of God's many wonderful gifts to be used in the service of others. So use your gift well." So yes, everyone (even you) has a gift that's supposed to be used to serve others. But don't get hung up on the word "service." It doesn't mean that you have to work for free like an indentured servant, never being rewarded for your labor. And that word "service" isn't restricted to serving in ministry or working at a church.

You serve others by bringing your multi-talented self fully to the table, boldly and unapologetically offering up the amazing gifts and abilities God has given you for His glory. You serve others by meeting practical needs and providing solutions, whether that's operating a daycare that provides a safe, loving learning environment for toddlers, or being a nationally recognized oncologist bringing hope and healing to as many cancer patients as possible. Each is an act of serving others in a way that leaves a lasting impact. But in order to show up that way, we must snatch our minds back from the self-doubt and insecurity that holds our purpose hostage. As hindering as self-doubt can be to living that vibrant, impactful

John 10:10 life Jesus promised us, from my observation historically the Christian community hasn't been all that helpful in building esteem in its members. As Christians, in our well-meaning effort to make sure that we don't succumb to pride (which God hates) and the various maladies it causes (it is deadly), we've often failed to develop a healthy, balanced view of what real confidence and true humility look like. As a result, as members of this community we often have a less than healthy view of our abilities and talents. In an effort to prevent pride, we've distorted the true definition of humility, which is simply not thinking you are better than other people. Notice, however, that humility isn't defined as thinking you are *worse* than other people. But somehow when we hear "humility" that falsity is exactly what many of us have internalized.

Just like we've distorted the meaning of humility, as believers we've also skewed the definition of pride as well. Some of us who are really confident in our abilities have been wrongly conditioned to believe that confidence equates to conceit. I love what author Jill M. Richardson says about pride: "Pride comes when we insist on establishing our superiority, not our capability. Pride exists when we take those gifts and use them for our agenda and glory.[55]" Superiority versus capability.

Wow! That distinction is so powerful and freeing because it allows us to

unabashedly own, declare and use our God-given, self-honed capabilities

to the fullest without offending God one tiny bit. It's only when we try to

use our gifts to make ourselves feel superior and others inferior that we get

the side eye from Jesus.

Because we misunderstand true humility and don't understand real

confidence, many of us don't believe we can be confident and humble at

the same time. I'm so grateful pastor and author Tim Keller sets us straight

on this one. In his book, "*The Reason for God: Belief in an Age of

Skepticism*," Keller writes, "The Christian gospel is that I am so flawed

that Jesus had to die for me, yet I am so loved and valued that Jesus was

glad to die for me. This leads to deep humility and deep confidence at the

same time.[56]"

If we're ever going to snatch back our minds from self-doubt, it's

imperative that we do two things: first, eradicate these unhealthy

---

[55] Jill M. Richardson, *"No Need to Downplay Your Leadership,"* Christianity Today, January 4, 2016. https://www.christianitytoday.com/women-leaders/2016/january/no-need-to-downplay-your-leadership.html

[56] Timothy Keller, p. 181.

distortions of what humility and pride are and second, embrace the truth that humility and confidence can and must co-exist in the life of an effective, impactful believer.

Real Confidence

In order to get a picture of what it looks like to have humility and confidence living side-by-side in the life of a believer, let's take at one of my favorite people in the whole Bible, David. If you're not familiar with David's story, you can read all about his life in 1 Samuel 16 through 2 Kings 2.

For anyone who knows his story well, descriptors of David that come to mind include worshipper, psalmist, king, shepherd boy, a man after God's own heart, even adulterer and murderer. However, David's best-known moniker is "giant killer." In today's vernacular, the phrase "David and Goliath" denotes a contest where a smaller, weaker opponent faces a much bigger, stronger adversary. Arguably, it's the most well-known underdog story of all time, used everywhere, from sports to business, to describe a contest with incredible odds.

David was just a young teen-aged shepherd out running an errand for his dad Jesse when the challenge of a lifetime divinely fell into his lap.

David's older brothers all served in the Israelite army under King Saul. The Israelites were at war with the Philistines when Jesse asked David to bring some food to his older brothers on the battlefield.

When David arrived at the Israelite campsite, he heard a ten foot tall giant by the name of Goliath talking smack about the Israelite army and their God. A common war-time practice in antiquity, Goliath challenged the Israelites to send one man out to fight him. And if Goliath won that one-on-one contest, the Israelites would become their slaves. But if the lone Israelite killed Goliath, the Philistines would serve the Israelites. As you might guess, there was a whole lotta hand-wringing going on in the Israelite camp: "You go fight him!" "No, you go!" "No way, man. I went last time!" Even King Saul, Israel's commander-in-chief and supposed fearless leader, was like, "Nah, bruh."

But when David arrived and heard Goliath's threats, righteous indignation rose up inside him. "David asked the soldiers standing nearby ... 'Who is this pagan Philistine anyway, that he is allowed to defy the armies of the living God?'"[57] Assessing that the very future of God's

---

[57] 1 Samuel 17:26, New Living Translation

chosen people was hanging in the balance, David knew what he had to do. As he prepared for the biggest fight of his young life, here's what David said as he implored King Saul for the opportunity to fight Goliath man to man:

> "'Don't worry about this Philistine,' David told Saul. *'I'll go fight him*!' 'Don't be ridiculous!' Saul replied. 'There's no way you can fight this Philistine and possibly win! You're only a boy, and he's been a man of war since his youth.' But David persisted. *'I have been taking care of my father's sheep and goats,'* he said. "When a lion or a bear comes to steal a lamb from the flock, *I go after it* with a club and rescue the lamb from its mouth. If the animal turns on me, *I catch it* by the jaw and club it to death. *I have done this* to both lions and bears, *and I'll do it* to this pagan Philistine, too, for he has defied the armies of the living God! The Lord who rescued me from the claws of the lion and the bear will rescue me from this Philistine!" Saul finally consented. "All right, go ahead," he said. "And may the Lord be with you![58]"

---

[58] 1 Samuel 17:32-38 New Living Translation, emphasis mine.

Ever notice how many "I" statements there are in that passage? I count six. Yeah, David eventually gets around to mentioning the Lord, but only after a pretty compelling synopsis of his qualifying credentials. And yet after being in church for over forty years, I've never once heard anyone ever describe David as "cocky," "arrogant," "proud," or "full of himself." Instead, we read David's self-pronouncements and instinctively want to give him a chest bump. Why? Sure, we all love it when a hero comes along (cue Mariah Carey), but something much more powerful is going on in this passage.

He may have just been a teenage kid at the time, but in this moment David is walking fully as the man God created him to be. In this confrontation with Goliath, David is unapologetically owning the gifts God has given him and boldly demonstrating the skills God has blessed him to acquire in his short lifetime. David's words and actions declared, "I was born to do this!"

David's confidence was not only fueled by his trust in God, but it was also reinforced by his self-talk. David had a life-long practice of encouraging himself. We see this in Psalm 18:29 where he courageously declares "In your strength I can crush an army; with my God I can scale any wall.[59]" Because of his self-talk, David held a picture of himself and a narrative true to his calling and capabilities. And David brought these to his remembrance to fuel his courage when facing challenges.

Who You Calling . . . ?

We might be tempted to think perhaps David's confidence came from being celebrated by his family. After all, the Bible says he was a gifted psalmist, an amazing worshipper, a skilled harpist, an extremely competent shepherd, and your boy handsome to boot. What's not to love, right?

But in reality David, as the youngest of Jesse's eight sons, was an after-thought. 1 Samuel 16 tells us that God directed Israel's Prophet Samuel to Jesse's house to anoint the next king of Israel from among Jesse's sons. When Samuel arrives, Jesse presents seven of his sons to Samuel with great anticipation that one of them will be the chosen one. Samuel looks them all over and asks, "Got anybody else?" Jesse replies "Uh . . . yeah. There's this other kid. Umm . . . somebody go out to the pasture and get . . . 'what's his name?'"

---

[59] New Living Translation

While David was forgotten by his own father, he never lost sight of who he was called by his Heavenly Father – chosen, valuable, capable and, most importantly, deeply loved. And through spending precious moments daily with God, David began to call himself just that. So when he showed up on that battlefield, David was fully clothed in his God-given identity. He didn't need to borrow Saul's armor.

One day when I was about six or seven years old, I stayed home from school because I was sick. Both my parents worked, so sick days were typically spent with either of my grandmothers taking care of me at their home. Full disclosure: "Sick days" usually meant I acted like I was dying until about ten o'clock in the morning, and then I would be miraculously healed and start asking grandma for all kinds of toys and things to eat.

This afternoon I had requested my Grandma Velma get me a moon pie and a doll. (For the uninitiated, moon pies are two round graham cracker cookies, with marshmallow filling in the center, dipped in a thick, flavored icing-like coating. Banana was my favorite. Hand-held diabetes.) As my Grandma Velma and I walked back from the store with my haul in hand, we approached a nearby elementary school. Classes were over and a big crowd of students had gathered around two kids who were fighting. Grandma Velma half seriously, half- joking chided them, asking "Now, why are y'all out here fightin' like this?" "Because he called me a name!" one of the boys yelled indignantly. My Grandma Velma just shook her head and said, "It's not what people call you, but what you answer to that matters."

Grandma Velma was on to something. I think she knew that what we say about ourselves is ultimately what we end up answering to. And whatever you answer to, in word or in deed, is what people will keep on calling you.

What David called himself was a major factor in his self-esteem quotient. It didn't matter that his brothers called him mischievous and a trouble-maker. It didn't matter that Saul called him inadequate and inexperienced. In making the case to Saul as to why he should be allowed to fight Goliath on all of Israel's behalf, David called himself capable, brave, prepared and covered. And as a result of what he called himself, David showed up on the battlefield to face Goliath supremely confident.

How would you show up in life – with your family, at work, amongst friends – if you snatched back your thoughts from self-doubt and began to call yourself something different from what you've been saying? How might your life change if you called yourself loved (1 John 3:1a), valuable (Matthew 6:26), unique (Psalm 139:13-14) and capable (Philippians 4:13), just as God has called you? What would happen if you refused to answer to anyone or any circumstance in life that called you less than what God has called you? What you answer to is what people will be forced to call you. But it all starts with what you call yourself.

When I was a college freshman at a predominately white institution, my English professor asked me to tutor a classmate. Neil, a young white male, was struggling with composition and sentence structure. I would spend hours going over his essays and other assignments with him. We both shared an interest in attending law school and would laugh skeptically about all the writing we'd have to do as attorneys.

No one in my family had ever attended law school, so I had no idea what to expect. To prepare myself, I spent most of my sophomore and junior years working in an African-American owned boutique law firm in downtown Atlanta, testing the waters and getting an idea of what being an attorney was like. The founding partner of the firm thought I had real potential and encouraged me to apply to law school.

In my junior year, I headed to the career office to discuss my post-graduate plans with my assigned counselor. She was a middle-aged white woman who was a very experienced career counselor, and she'd been assigned to me because graduate school was her specialty. I was hoping to get her recommendation on which law schools to apply to and get some guidance on taking the law school aptitude test (the LSAT).

I sat down so excited about my future, only to leave dejected. After spending less than ten minutes with me, she coolly said, "If I were you, I'd rethink going to law school. Maybe pursue a career as a paralegal for a while instead. Law school is very demanding and requires a ton of analysis and logical thinking. And so does the LSAT. You should take some time to work on those skills before you apply. And then, *maybe* you can look at some second tier schools." I walked back to my dorm room confused and angry.

About a week later, I was walking in one of the main buildings headed to class when I approached a group of students huddled in conversation. I overheard one of them very matter-of-factly say, "Yeah, I just got accepted to UVA's law school." Neil and I had lost touch since freshman year, but I still recognized that voice. My head spun around like Linda Blair in *The Exorcist*.

When I saw Neil later that day in the student center, I asked him about his process of applying to law schools and his experience with the college's career counseling office. Turns out that although my grade point average was higher than his, the very same counselor who had discouraged me had been extremely supportive of Neil in his quest to attend law school. I walked away from my conversation with Neil thinking, "How the hell did *he* even get into law school? And who the hell is this woman to tell me I can't make it, but encourage him when *I* had to tutor *his* dumb a$$?" As I mulled the whole thing over in my mind, I let a few additional expletives fly. Listen: I was a cussing Christian. I was saved, but clearly not yet sanctified.

Sadly, my experience wasn't unique at all. Still today, students of color at predominantly white institutions are still facing these kinds of ugly, belittling encounters. But as hurtful as that experience was, it taught me a very valuable lesson.

Around that time, there was a song recorded by a popular gospel choir. During the chorus, the tenors would sing, "Whose report will you believe?" and the altos and sopranos would jubilantly and emphatically respond, "We shall believe the report of the Lord!" That day I had to decide whose report I was going to believe. Was I going to believe the "experienced" career counselor who said I wasn't smart enough to make it through law school? Or was I going to believe that I was intelligent, capable, full of potential and could do all things through Christ?

By this time Grandma Velma had been in heaven for about six years, but I could still hear her words ringing in my head. What name was I going to answer to? Was I going to answer to the label of "second class student" and trash my law school plans? Or was I going to answer to "conqueror" and pursue a career as an attorney?

Not only did I apply to law school, but I did really well on the LSAT. In fact, I scored high enough to be accepted to my alma mater, New York University School of Law, one of the top ten law schools in the country. No second tier school for this chick.

Each of us will have numerous situations in our lives that will call into question who we are. What we call ourselves will ultimately determine how we respond and, most importantly, whether we live our preferred John 10:10 life.

Do Your Work

Ever feel like the woman from my workshop? You know, the one who struggled with self-doubt and a lack of confidence? If so, it's time to snatch your thoughts back. Turn to Section 6 of The Snatch Back Notebook and complete the exercises there.

Now, in Section Two of this book, we'll dive into the second major area I addressed in order to execute my own Operation Snatch Back – reclaiming my time.

PART II

Reclaim Your Time

Chapter 7

Maximizing Every Moment

I absolutely love my own birthday. I do a little something to celebrate every day during my birthday month, and for milestone birthdays I celebrate all year. And getting older hasn't deterred me one bit. In fact, many years ago I adopted my late Grandpa Matt's saying as my mantra: "The only way not to get old is to die young." So as someone who's lost a few very close friends all under the age of 50, I tell my age proudly, grateful I haven't died young.

But I'm not satisfied to just be here. My personal formula for happiness is to live, laugh, love, learn and earn. And every year on my birthday, I take the time to reflect on my living, laughing, loving, learning and earning, deciding how to improve each aspect of my life. Over the years, I've used my birthday as a catalyst for everything from getting into shape to mastering a new skill.

I'm not sure whether it's the realization that you have more runway behind you than in front of you or that you've lived long enough to become more secure in who you are, but there was something different about approaching fifty. It was on my forty-eighth birthday in March 2017 that I began seriously reevaluating my life. My family had buried my older brother Duane just three months earlier, so that year's birthday assessment had a pronounced, solemn tone.

When Duane died suddenly in January 2017, profound changes began to take place in how I viewed my life, my time and my purpose. Only fifty-one years old when he died, Duane was intelligent, engaging, well-read, charismatic, handsome and gregarious. A father, husband, Ph.D. candidate and decorated senior law enforcement officer who was beloved and respected by so many, his untimely death left our family and community stunned.

An avid gym rat, Duane was in great physical shape when his car was hit by a drunk driver. Although he survived the accident with minor injuries, a medication that he was taking for a resulting shoulder injury left him with an arrhythmia. As a result of complications resulting from a fairly routine cardiac procedure undertaken to address the arrhythmia, Duane lapsed into a coma.

I rushed from my home in New Jersey to New Orleans to see Duane, and be with our mother and his wife and children. The entire family gathered at the hospital day after day, praying and waiting, taking turns staying with Duane overnight. On one of those nights, I sat up with Duane reading scriptures, praying over him and singing worship songs. Around 3 o'clock in the morning, I noticed unusual activity on the heart rate monitor. I called for the nurse and, in what seemed like a matter of nanoseconds, a code blue was called, with hospital personnel rushing in from everywhere on the floor. It felt like I was in a scene from a TV drama.

I witnessed the violence Duane's body underwent as the medical staff tried to resuscitate him. And although he would survive this episode, Duane eventually died a couple days later after a series of heart attacks.

My brother's death impacted me in ways I still struggle to articulate, even years later. Besides being outraged that his life was cut short due to a surgeon's mistake, another reaction I had to Duane's death was to become very contemplative about my life's work. Duane had spent all of his adult life working in law enforcement, and he absolutely loved it.

Not only did Duane thrive professionally, but he also left an imprint on others personally.

From inspiring his officers to complete their college degrees to praying for a close friend of his through a divorce, Duane left an indelible imprint. On the day of his funeral, officer after officer told stories of the profound impact my brother had on their lives, making them better officers and better people. Although his life was cut short and he had his share of personal challenges, I believe Duane still lived a John 10:10 life – a rich, satisfying life of purpose, impact and vitality.

When I think of all that he accomplished, Ephesians 5:11-16 comes to mind, which says *"Don't waste your time* on useless work, mere busywork . . . So watch your step. Use your head. *Make the most of every chance you get.*[60]" While I never thought I had all the time in the world to fulfill my God-given purpose, Duane's death created a deeper yearning in me to make the most of every moment.

Shortly after Duane died, I began feeling stagnant professionally, like I needed a new challenge. I knew my purpose was to serve and

---

[60] The Message Bible

develop others into greatness. I had a tribe of Spirit-filled, bright, forward-thinking men and women who were some of my biggest prayer warriors and cheerleaders, and I held a role leading people I really loved.

But I still felt stagnant. I wanted to use the full complement of skills God had blessed me to acquire over my lifetime. I'd sat in Corporate America for years believing God wanted me to invest the experience He was allowing me to gain into building His kingdom, only to face the disheartening reality that local church environments were often less than receptive. Additionally, it became clear to me that I needed to develop and learn in ways I currently wasn't. I also couldn't shake my desire to impact people in a broader way than I was currently doing in my local church. I began to have an overwhelming sense that God wanted me to extend my reach beyond those four walls. I could feel a push in my spirit to maximize every moment.

So on my birthday in March 2017, I decided to do for myself what I'd done for others as an executive strategist: I figured out my next best move. I allowed my mind to step out of my past career experiences (finance and law), my present environment (faith-based) and my current role (pastoring). By mentally stepping away from these things, I gave myself the gifts of the permission and space to dream.

Starting with a blank sheet of paper, I began the process of coaching myself through one of the most meaningful and rewarding professional transitions of my life. But I didn't start with a list of possible jobs or careers for which I might be qualified. I started with two much deeper questions: *who* was I and *where* was I?

Who Are You, Really?

I was born Monique Christine Carkum, the youngest child of Curtis & Bernice Carkum. Carkum is a rather unusual surname, and in New Orleans where I grew up my immediate family were the only ones. My parents, particularly my father, were fairly well-known. So on more occasions than I can count, when I would give my full name whether at school or applying for a job, I would invariably be asked, "Carkum? You Curtis/Bernice's lil girl?" And if the last name weren't enough, I looked just like my mother looked when she was growing up. As older siblings are prone to do, mine used to tease me, telling me I was adopted. Nice try y'all, but I knew better because I looked too much like Mama. If there was ever a question about to whom I belonged, my looks and last name told the whole story. Both of my parents were educators, and all of my siblings were highly intelligent and had great academic promise. So as I followed them in school, academic success was expected of me. Why? You guessed it. That last name. No matter whom I wanted to be, I was a Carkum. And that was that.

Just like our surnames, inherited physical features and family standards define who we are, so does our God-given purpose. So, who are you, really? Remember that life purpose statement I asked you to develop in Chapter 1? Pull it out.

Your life purpose statement is to be lived out, not just read. So take the time to really reflect on it. How consistently are you living your life purpose? Are you consistently showing up as the gift to the world God designed you to be? Or have life circumstances robbed you of your purpose, vitality and impact? And if so, to what degree have those things been stolen? Are we talking simple breaking and entering, or armed robbery with assault?

Undergirding our life purpose are our personal values. Our values reflect who we really are, not who we'd like to be or how we prefer to be perceived by others. Our values serve as goalposts for our lives: we feel

THE SNATCH BACK: RECLAIMING YOUR LIFE ONE TRUTH AT A TIME

aligned, fulfilled and productive when we live within them. Conversely, we feel diminished and unsuccessful when we live outside of them.

At times, we may need to course-correct to ensure we're spending our time in ways that most honor our values. Many times when we feel "off" or out of balance it's because we've compromised our values in some way. The compromise doesn't have to be as drastic as some unethical decision or immoral action. Dissonance rises to the surface when we do something as simple as spending way too much time at work when relationships with family and friends is a core value.

Because our society wears busyness as a badge of honor, we often find it difficult to say no, allowing ourselves to get pulled into all kinds of things. These things may be good – but if they don't align with our values, they're not good for *us*. Getting clear on your values helps you determine which options, amongst all the good ones for spending your time, are the right ones for you. Getting clear on your values will help you remember who you are.

Do Your Work

Take some time to clarify your values by asking yourself: "What's really important to me? What must be present in my life in order to feel fulfilled? What are my non-negotiables?" In The Snatch Back Notebook you'll find a framework in Section 7 to complete your values clarification exercise.

Where Are You, Really?

Making the most of our time requires you to evaluate not only who you are, but also *where* you are. You may be sitting in your living room, your neighborhood coffee shop or your office reading this book. But where are you, really? Not your current physical location, but on this journey called life.

Making the most of our time requires that we make a brutally honest assessment about the life season we're in. More important than whether you're a young adult or Baby Boomer, a millennial or a Gen-Xer, the season of life you're in has less to do with age and more to do with seasons of purpose. Are you in a season of tilling soil and planting seeds of opportunity to fulfill your purpose? Are you in a season of reaping the harvest from years of sowing time and energy to develop your gifts? Could you be in a summer season of rest and relaxation, enjoying the fruit of the hard work you've put in to honing your talents? Maybe you're shivering in the winter of adversity, trying to figure out exactly what you've been called to do.

The season of your life will have a great impact on how you redeem, or make the most of, your time. If you're in a season of building your career, your time may be best invested attending grad school, so you'll have to sow seeds of preparation. This means other activities may have to be curtailed for a while. If you're in the process of expanding your business, meetings with investors and networking with potential partners may take priority over leisure. Just like it'd be absurd to wear a wool coat to a swimming pool in the summertime, when we fail to allocate our time based on our season of life we can end up looking pretty silly. If you're going to truly make the most of every chance you get as Ephesians 5:16 encourages us to do, you'll need to examine closely the season of life you're currently in and make adjustments to how you spend your time accordingly.

In March 2017, as I sat with my blank piece of paper, I began to reflect on who I really was. I thought about my upbringing, my young adulthood and my current season of life. I thought about the life experiences, both personal and professional, that had shaped me. I began to jot down the adjectives I thought best described me currently. Then I took a hard look at where I was. As I reflected on my particular season of life, I wrote down the amount of time on average I spent each day engaged in certain activities. Then I jotted down the values that I hold dearest. A quick comparison showed that while I claimed to value certain things like family and my own spiritual growth, my calendar told a different story. And the way I described myself – dynamic, courageous and Spirit-filled – wasn't how I was consistently showing up. So when I pulled out my life purpose statement to evaluate how consistent it was (or wasn't) with the life I was now living, I knew some changes were in order if I was going to live a life congruent with who I was created to be.

Do Your Work

As you endeavor to make the most of the time God has granted you, take some time to answer a few questions about who you are and where you are in Section 7 of The Snatch Back Notebook.

Who You Calling an Elephant?

After I sat down on my birthday and really evaluated my season of life, my values, how I was showing up and my life purpose statement, I knew I had to make some changes. But I wasn't entirely sure where to start.

Dreaming is one thing. Doing is a whole 'nother thing. I'd love to tell you I spent a weekend sequestered away in deep reflection, and thereafter emerged with crystal clarity and the fortitude to press send on my resignation email. But that'd be a big ole lie.

The day after my birthday, life resumed at its normal frenetic pace. And before I knew it, I was back to scheduling counseling sessions with church members, leading ministries, managing my kids' after school activities and accompanying Lennon to his professional events. And while I was busy, busyness wasn't the only thing that kept me from taking that next step. I would spend the next few months internally grappling with something much bigger.

"You're freer than you think you are." Those words jumped off the page and backhand slapped the daylights out of me. Amidst the hustle and bustle of work and family, I did manage to carve out some small pockets of time for myself. During this precious downtime, that one sentence from a book I was reading challenged my entire thought process about what my next move should be. The crazy thing was I had started reading this same book four years earlier, but had never finished it. But alas, when the student is ready the teacher will appear.

I would spend the months following my birthday thinking of ways to address the old nagging feelings of stagnation and the new feelings of frustration that were starting to bubble up within me. And while I'm known for pushing people to think higher, see bigger and believe greater for their personal and professional lives, I have to confess I was still thinking small about my own at this point. I had toyed with the idea of attending seminary for years, so I began researching schools and speaking with some pastors who were seminary grads and whose opinions I respected. I figured as a pastor, attending seminary was the logical thing to do, so I took a class hoping that would spark some transformation.

But as much as I love studying the Bible, seminary didn't excite me or ignite any hunger in me for more. I even found a fun and exciting opportunity that offered a lot of growth with a learning and development company. But that role would have required me to walk away from my current one. I kept trying to think of ways to stay in my current role while obeying the leading I was feeling. I was living as a hypocrite of sorts - through my ministry I was cheering hundreds of people on to higher, bigger and greater pursuits for their lives, while trying to make only small, non-disruptive changes in my own.

Making the most of your time not only requires that you know who you are and what season of life you're in. It also means taking a good hard look at why you've made the choices you have regarding how you spend your time and where you invest your gifts.

Any Christian worth his "Honk if you love Jesus" bumper sticker knows John 8:36: "If the Son sets you free, you will be free indeed.[61]" So it's rare that we would ever question the efficacy of Christ's sacrifice at Calvary to indeed set us free spiritually. But what about Christ setting us free to live here on earth the rich and satisfying life He promised us in John 10:10? Whether we realize it or not, how we spend our time and where we invest our energy speaks volumes about whether or not we really believe God has a preferred life designed for us.

The choices we make about how to spend our time also reveal whether we feel the freedom to pursue that John 10:10 life. We have God's promise in Romans 8:32 which says, "Since he did not spare even his own Son but gave him up for us all, won't he also give us everything else?[62]" So along with our salvation comes God's promise that He'll give

---

[61] New International Version
[62] New Living Translation

us everything we need to live out the rich and satisfying life He desires for us. And yet we stand at the gate of life like the circus elephant with a rope around its neck. The folklore tale of how circus elephants are trained goes like this:

When baby elephants are still (relatively) small, a strong rope is tied around their necks and attached to a well-grounded pole. When the baby elephant tries to walk away, the resistance of the rope attached to the pole prevents the baby elephant from doing so. Over time, after numerous unsuccessful attempts to break free, the baby elephant realizes it just isn't strong enough. So it stops pulling on the rope, and stays put. Eventually when the trainer places the rope over the baby elephant's head, it no longer resists because the baby elephant has been conditioned to believe it can't break free. The baby elephant has become so domesticated that the trainer doesn't have to even attach the rope to the secured pole. She can control the baby elephant with just the rope alone. Over time the baby elephant grows, and while it's undoubtedly physically strong enough to break free from any restraint, it's mentally conditioned to believe resistance is futile. So the adult circus elephant stays put.

The elephant clearly doesn't recognize its power. With one half-hearted head jerk, the elephant can free itself of all constraints. That elephant is freer than it thinks. Just like that elephant, we each have the power to break free from the mental and emotional constraints that hold us back from fulfilling our purpose, living with vitality and having incredible impact, but many of us have been conditioned by life to think we can't. So we stay chained to thoughts, feelings and actions that keep us living devoid of those things. Why? Like the adult elephant with the rope around its neck that could be so easily broken, we remain tied to people, situations and circumstances that restrict our progress. And all the while time is just tick, tick, ticking away.

But wait. . . didn't the Son set us free indeed? Of course we know He did according to John 8:36. So in reality, we really are freer than we think. But since our thoughts dictate our feelings, our feelings influence our actions and our actions determine our outcomes, *we behave only as free as we think we are.* And when we believe we're stuck, we fail to take the steps that would allow us to make the most of our time.

I know this all too well because for almost two decades I stayed trapped in a career that wasn't my calling. For years, I fantasized about

162

escaping the practice of law, but somehow I always allowed some impediment, real or imagined, to hold me back. Once I was able to break free from that, it took me another five years to fully go after what I was put on this earth to do. And what was I doing during those five years? Lots of meaningful, eternally worthwhile work in ministry, for sure. But I was also tiptoeing around my purpose instead of diving in to it head first. And while I was side-stepping tough decisions about my future, time was ticking away. It'd take a life-altering encounter before I would eventually dive in headfirst.

Chapter 8

Honor Your Time

"How in the world did we accumulate all this stuff?" I asked no one in particular for the 856th time as we cleaned out our basement. It was August 2017 and we'd just returned from our family vacation to Milan. It was on the seven hour plane ride that I got inspired to tackle the hard stuff in my life after reading one of those "Girl, get your life together" books. Our overrun basement somehow made it to the top of the list of things holding me back from living my best life and robbing me of my greatness.

So I conscripted Lennon, the kids and our poor babysitter Junie into one week of hard labor. At least Lennon got to leave to go to work. The kids would help a little (and I mean very little) and then disappear for hours on end. I threatened to withhold food and motherly affection, but Brooklynn and Judah decided to take their chances. My screams for help fell on deaf, hiding ears, leaving Junie and me to do the heavy lifting.

Around day four, Junie and I were killing it when we reached the anathema of my very existence aka the storage room. It was then that I wished I'd just slept on the plane ride back from Italy. Filled with boxes from when we moved in ten years prior, our storage room was full of random stuff we just didn't feel like dealing with. It was so packed you could barely open the door, but when you put an attorney and a medical school student (that would be Junie) together, you get the kind of tenacity that puts the lives of the elderly and small children in jeopardy. Until the task is done, no one is safe.

As I slogged through what seemed to be the hundredth box of old books and papers, I came across the consent forms for a cardiac procedure I'd undergone over ten years prior. Since my early twenties, I'd experienced random episodes of rapidly accelerated heart rate. With no rhyme or reason, my heart would suddenly start beating like I was in an aerobics class. No amount of deep breathing, lying down or any other relaxation technique would help. These episodes would last for up to thirty minutes, stopping just as suddenly as they started, leaving me physically drained. And scared. They occurred frequently enough for me to recognize

THE SNATCH BACK: RECLAIMING YOUR LIFE ONE TRUTH AT A TIME

the symptoms but not frequently enough to be captured by the heart monitor I wore from time to time over the years.

Fortuitously, while in the hospital recovering after delivering Brooklynn, I had an episode. I frantically pressed the nurse call button and summoned a doctor. I was placed on an EKG machine and seen by a cardiologist who diagnosed me as having a type of heart arrhythmia. I was given the option of having a procedure performed to correct it or trying to manage my condition with medication. I chose medication, but after a few years its efficacy waned. My cardiologist strongly advised me to have the procedure done before having our next child so that I'd eliminate the risk of having an episode during labor and delivery. The procedure was performed successfully and without complications. I was finally able to live my life free from the years of fear and uncertainty my arrhythmia had caused. Best decision ever.

Ten years later as I stood in my storage room holding the consent form for the cardiac procedure, I read through all the potential risks. A few words jumped off the page and locked onto my heart with a vise grip. I was speechless as I read the words that described the very complications my brother Duane, who'd undergone a similar procedure, had died from.

As I stood in my storage room holding that paperwork, I began to have an overwhelming sense of God's presence in my life and His purpose for my life. Simply put, I had been spared from what had killed my brother.

From March 2017 to August 2017, I'd spent five months ruminating off and on over the need to make a career change. In addition to taking a seminary class, I also studied leadership and change management through an online course offered by MIT. Surprisingly, I loved it way more than I had my seminary class. While I wasn't exactly sure what career direction to go in, one thing was clear: my current role wasn't working anymore. But I just hadn't found the courage to leave it behind. So I'd allow myself to get distracted by the busyness and tell myself I'd figure it all out "later." Prior to my basement epiphany I hadn't been ready mentally or emotionally to make major moves, but now I was.

While I enjoyed preaching and counseling as an executive pastor, what I loved most was developing key leadership skills in the directors of the numerous ministries I oversaw. One of my favorite things about my role was identifying growth opportunities in new leaders and designing an approach to ministry leadership that would intentionally facilitate their progress in those areas. Observing someone perform beneath their potential had always been disheartening for me. But following my

basement epiphany, witnessing under-utilized or under-developed

potential in others began to irk me like never before. Every time I

observed what I thought was someone failing to maximize their time,

making excuses or squandering their gift, I had to restrain myself from

grabbing them by the collar and screaming in their face, "Stop playing and

get it together! You don't have as much time as you think!" These

moments taught me that a big part of my John 10:10 life would be to serve

as a more powerful catalyst for professional growth and achievement in

others. I just needed to figure out how to do it in a way that wouldn't get

me slapped with an assault charge.

So starting in September 2017, I entered into a ninety day season

of praying and fasting intermittently, asking God to show me "what next."

Out Of The Mouths Of Babes

When we ask God to speak to our hearts and provide direction, we often

do so with assumptions, preconceived notions and limitations. I entered

my season of prayer and fasting looking for God to speak to me about my

calling as it related to my career. But God had another area of calling he

wanted to address.

It was our daughter Brooklynn's thirteenth birthday in November of 2017. I'd been at the church since before 7 o'clock that morning overseeing our annual food give away event, filling in for another leader who had a death in the family. After spending the entire day at church, I raced home to drive Brooklynn and six of her closest girlfriends to a sleepover at Great Wolf Lodge, an indoor water park resort in the Poconos.

After a late dinner, while Brooklynn and her friends went back to the water slides sans her little brother, Judah sat eating his dessert while I checked messages on my phone. "Mama, are you still working?" Judah asked. "No, not anymore," I said, hastily putting my phone away. Then Judah proceeded to say something I'll never forget. "Mama, people are always texting you and calling you. Can't they call somebody else? You work so much, and you're always tired. And I'm starting to resent the church." Not at all what I was expecting. I tried to gather myself. "So . . . um, Judah . . . when you say 'resent the church,' do you mean resent going to church? Or do you mean resent the people at the church?" I was afraid of his answer, but deep down I knew what was coming next. "I'm starting to resent the *people*, Mama."

Ten year old Judah had rocked my world. Our kids loved our local church family, having been there practically all their lives. Lennon and I never had any resistance from them on Sundays or any other day - they always went willingly and happily to every event. Or so I'd thought. So to say I was shocked to hear these words would be an understatement.

We'd sprung for a huge room with an upstairs loft for the birthday girl and her crew, while Lennon and Judah shared a room down the hall. As the girls stayed up until the wee hours of the morning laughing and talking, I laid wide awake in the upstairs bedroom replaying the conversation with Judah over and over in my mind. Then I overheard Natalia, one of Brooklynn's best friends, ask "Brooklynn, is your mom okay? She looked so tired at dinner tonight." "Yeah," Brooklynn replied, "my mom's always tired. I'm worried about her." Another knife in my heart.

I'd always said that, as a pastor, my kids were my first congregation. How could my children be feeling this way and I not know it? How had I missed the signs? Later when I asked Brooklynn why she'd never said anything before about how she was feeling, her response was,

"Mommy, I didn't want to take something away from you that you loved so much."

At that point my ninety day fast wasn't scheduled to be over for another month, but I already had my answer. That Sunday morning on the drive back home to New Jersey, while the girls belted out the songs on Brooklynn's playlist, I played over and over in my mind the hard decisions I knew I'd have to make and the tough conversations that would follow.

I mentioned that earlier in 2017 I'd found another job I'd briefly considered taking. It was as an executive coach for an international learning and development company. As one of their coaches, I would work with professionals from a broad range of industries on honing their leadership skills, using a rather unique training approach. After interviewing extensively with the company, they'd left the ball in my court. But as a way to avoid making a tough decision, I had simply never followed through with it. During this time of fasting and praying, I felt God tapping me on the shoulder, reminding me of that opportunity. It offered me just the right combination of learning, challenge, growth and reward, all while helping others win professionally. Most importantly, I'd work only a couple days each month, leaving lots of time for Brooklynn and Judah. They'd be so happy. So I rekindled my conversations with the head of their coaching department, and found that due to increased demand for coaches with my background, they were still very much interested in me.

Lennon and I gathered the kids and announced that I'd be making some job changes so I could work less and spend more time with them. They were beyond thrilled. While I didn't give them details, I promised change by the new year. While we always discuss and make decisions as a family, I had another reason for telling my kids. Ever made a promise to a child? Ever not fulfilled that promise? Yeah, not pretty. I had given Brooklynn and Judah my word, so was now committed on another level to following through with those changes.

After months of stalling, I was finally ready emotionally and mentally to move. The holidays were approaching, so I decided to have a conversation with my lead pastor after Christmas about my plans and transitioning my role over time. For the first time in months, I felt clarity and peace about the direction I was headed in. I was overjoyed!

But in mid-December 2017, less than a week after finally making the decision to leave, an unexpected, unwelcomed event required me to stay in place for longer than I had planned. My lead pastor went on personal leave, and our church entered a period of unprecedented turmoil. With no other pastors on staff at our church, running the day to day operations fell to me. I went from an already full plate to a buffet table that included all my current duties, plus preaching two services on Sundays, leading our mid-week prayer service, additional counseling sessions and hospital visits, and long, late night board meetings. I put the coaching opportunity on hold as long as I could, but after two months of delay the folks at my new gig needed a firm commitment. Unable to give them one, I reluctantly had to let that opportunity go.

Meanwhile, between work and home responsibilities, I was burning the candle at both ends and in the middle. The stress I was under during those months took such a toll I lost almost fifteen pounds. When I unbraided my hair, clumps fell out. I would awaken every night around 3:00 a.m. having what I now realize were panic attacks.

Always mentally quick and verbally facile, I began to have difficulty collecting my thoughts and conversation was laborious. I recall

THE SNATCH BACK: RECLAIMING YOUR LIFE ONE TRUTH AT A TIME

one afternoon during this time I was having a conversation with my financial advisor Anthony regarding investment decisions. I couldn't follow his explanations about the money moves he wanted to make. For twenty years I had handled our family's finances. Now I sheepishly had to ask Anthony to call Lennon instead. I just couldn't process what he was saying to me. I called my sister Shelly and burst into tears. "I literally can't even think straight any more!" I cried.

Just as things were coming to a head, one evening in February 2018 I collapsed in the foyer of my home unable to move my arms and struggling to speak. "Get her to the ER *immediately*! We need to rule out the possibility of a stroke." I was conscious and could hear my doctor through the cell phone Lennon was holding as he bent over me. With Lennon and the kids standing over me praying, I immediately thought of how in the final days of his life my brother Duane had collapsed in his home before being taken to the hospital. The fear that gripped me was indescribable. As a believer in Jesus Christ, I believe my eternal salvation is secure. So I wasn't afraid to die.

In that moment, *I was afraid that I hadn't really lived.*

Criminally Cautious

In Matthew 25:14-30, Jesus gives the parable of the talents. In this parable, Jesus describes a master who goes away on a trip. Before he leaves, he entrusts certain sums of money to each of his servants. He gives one servant five talents, to another he gives two talents, and to the third servant he gives a single talent. The first two servants make wise investments, doubling the money given to them. When the master returns, these two servants each give him the original investment and the profit they earned. The master applauds them for their efforts, "His master replied, 'Well done, good and faithful servant! You have been faithful with a few things; I will put you in charge of many things. Come and share your master's happiness!'"

The third servant, however, buries his talent out in a field instead of trying to make a profit. When the master asks for an accounting, this servant says, "See, what had happened was . . ." Well, not exactly, but close enough:

"'Master, I know you have high standards and hate careless ways, that you demand the best and make no allowances for error. I was *afraid* I might disappoint you, so I found a good *hiding place* and secured your

money. Here it is, safe and sound down to the last cent.'"[63]

This servant tells his master, "I didn't even try because I was afraid

to fail. So I hid the talent you gave me." Note the master in this parable

doesn't say, "Oh, you poor thing. I know how risky and stressful the stock

market can be. No worries." Jesus says in Matthew 25:26-30, "The master

was furious. 'That's a terrible way to live! *It's criminal to live cautiously*

like that! If you knew I was after the best, why did you do less than the

least? The least you could have done would have been to invest the sum

with the bankers, where at least I would have gotten a little interest. Take

the [talent] and give it to the one who risked the most. And *get rid of this*

"play-it-safe" who won't go out on a limb. Throw him out into utter

darkness.'"[64]

There are several different interpretations about the lesson Jesus is

trying to teach His disciples through this parable of the talents. While

some Bible scholars believe Jesus is teaching about preparation for His

imminent return, I agree with the view that this parable is primarily a

---

[63] Matthew 25:24-25, emphasis mine.
[64] The Message Bible, emphasis mine.

lesson in stewardship. The bottom line is we're responsible for what we do with what God has given us. The third servant's failure wasn't so much that he wasted the master's money. His transgression was that *he wasted an opportunity*.

What caused the servant to waste that opportunity? Matthew 25:25 tells us it was fear. This servant played it so safe, he never even got in the game. And while he didn't lose anything, he didn't gain anything either. As a result, his caution was characterized by Jesus as "criminal." C'mon Jesus, criminal? Really? That's some pretty strong language. But Jesus doesn't say what He doesn't mean. Could it be that when we let fear hold us back from living a life of purpose, vitality and impact we're committing the crime of robbing others of the glory God wants to display through us and the blessing He wants us to be to those around us?

On the ride to the hospital that night in February 2018, I reflected on where I was in my life. At that point, I'd felt for almost a year that God wanted me to pursue a different career, but I kept allowing all the "what ifs" to trip me up. For months, I had privately battled guilt and self-doubt, wondering if my growing desires for change were rooted in the flesh and not the Spirit. I struggled with a sense of duty and obligation, worrying over who would pick up the things at the church that I'd inevitably leave behind. And although I didn't earn much money and wasn't by any means my family's primary bread-winner, I still worried about not having a steady paycheck.

I was also nervous because I frankly had no clue how to tackle the speaking and writing careers I sensed God wanted me to pursue. When I moved into ministry full-time I was so convinced the local church was where I was supposed to be that I'd allowed just about all of my corporate contacts to lapse. I had been so immersed in ministry for the past five years that now my network consisted primarily of the couple hundred people at my local church, and a few other small churches that were familiar with my preaching. I'd left a lucrative corporate career to start from the bottom in ministry, only to now feel led to leave ministry to pursue other endeavors with no clear route on how to get there and no contacts to speak of. Thanks a lot, Jesus.

For months I had turned these concerns over in my mind again and again. What I was calling "prayerful analysis" was just thinly veiled fear. But then I'd *finally* made a decision to move out in faith, only to be met with a life-threatening delay. Now, as I waited at the hospital to have a variety of neurological tests run, I had to admit to myself that I'd been criminally cautious.

As I was being guided into the MRI scanner, I remembered how my brother Duane had fallen into a coma while in the very same type of apparatus and never regained consciousness. As the hospital technician guided me into the scanner, I prayed a silent prayer, *"God, please don't let me die here."* To be clear, I wasn't afraid of dying. I was afraid to die *"here"*.

"Here" wasn't a physical location. "Here" wasn't the hospital. "Here" was this place I had allowed myself to get to in life where my purpose had been warped, vitality had been sucked out of me and my impact had been diminished. So right then and there in the MRI machine, I made a vow to the Lord, that if He got me out of there alive, I was going to really live. I was going to honor the time He had given me by moving faithfully toward what He had for me. No more playing it safe.

Once I was released from the hospital, I was placed on several weeks of medical leave while I underwent further neurological testing. Thankfully, the neurologist concluded that my episode was stress-induced and nothing more severe. The medical leave gave me plenty of time to rest and recover. With lots of encouragement from Lennon and the kids, I mastered the art of doing nothing. I slept for hours on end. Slowly my appetite returned and I began to eat again.

During my medical leave in March 2018, I turned forty-nine years old. To celebrate, Lennon had arranged a Caribbean cruise with our life-long best friends Oz and Lisa. After getting clearance from my neurologist to travel, I hopped aboard. The weather sucked and we weren't able to port in a few of the locations, so we spent almost the entire time trapped on the ship. Other passengers complained, but me? It had been exactly one year since I first sat down and began the process of transitioning my career, and two weeks since my collapse. I was happy to just be alive and recovering.

One morning on the cruise as I sat on the deck having devotional time, I came across two scriptures that really spoke to my heart:

"As long as it is day, we must do the works of him who sent me. Night is coming, when no one can work."[65]

---

[65] John 9:4, New International Version

"What do you know about tomorrow? How can you be so sure about your life? It is nothing more than mist that appears for only a little while before it disappears."[66]

From March 2017 to August 2017, I'd spent five months mulling over whether I should make career changes. Once I had my basement epiphany that August and definitely decided in November to make moves, I'd put off giving notice until after the Christmas holidays. Here I was in March 2018. All of my decisions in the past year had been based on the premise that I had time. And now a year later as I sat on that cruise ship, I'd come face to face with the reality that I didn't.

Eventually my cognitive processing was restored and my speech pattern was rapid-fire once again. But most importantly, those weeks of rest brought unusual clarity about what God *didn't* want me doing in this season of my life. And with that clarity came a resolve and commitment that I had previously lacked. I was so grateful to be alive, I wasn't going to

---

[66] James 4:14, Contemporary English Version

squander another second. And I was ready to honor the time God had so graciously extended to me here on this earth. I was ready to snatch my life back.

Although at the end of my medical leave I very briefly resumed my normal responsibilities at the church, I was anything but. I returned with a fire in me that had never burned quite so bright and hot before. Once our minds and hearts have been enlarged to see the expansive vision God has for our lives, it becomes almost impossible to fit back into the organizational constructs, relationship dynamics and paradigms that we once tolerated or even embraced. Like a baby whose time has come, we just can't stay where we are. And once we've been delivered, we can't fit back into the womb, try as we might.

Where I'd previously been reluctant to take risks, now I was ready to set a match and some lighter fluid to "safe." Deep down, my desire was to find work that allowed me to love and serve others (The Greatest Commandment found in Luke 10:27) while making the highest and best use of my gifts and talents, and fulfilling Jesus' commandment to share the Gospel (The Great Commission found in Matthew 28:1-20). And I wanted to do it while having enough time for my first and most important congregation – my family. For the first time in years, I began to wholeheartedly embrace a vision of a full-time career *outside* of local church ministry. I imagined what my days would look like as a coach, speaker and writer, and the broader impact I could have for God's kingdom. I began to see how pursuing those careers didn't have to mean I was leaving ministry. Those opportunities could mean *broader* ministry.

Faith Walk or Reality Check?

But while being a coach, speaker and writer sounded wonderful, I had no coaching clients, no audience outside of my small local church, and had never written anything other than sermons and legal briefs. That was a hard reality check. I wasn't a hundred percent sure what God wanted me to do next, but I knew I couldn't stay where I was. I reached out to the learning and development company that had previously offered me a position, only to learn that, while they were still very interested in me, they wouldn't be bringing any new coaches on for at least another nine months.

Although I had no idea what else to do, I knew if I stayed in my current role much longer, I'd lose my will to make the tough decision. So without a clear game plan, I resigned from my position at my local church. I began to see my reality check as a faith walk.

Within a few days of my resignation, Jamila, one of the young adult professionals in my church, contacted me asking if I could recommend a career coach for her. Over the years as she attended the life group I led in my home, we had lots of discussions about her career development, promotion opportunities and office politics. When I reported back to her that I was unable to find one, she said, "Pastor Monique, why don't *you* just coach me?" And with that, I started Gravitas, my own executive coaching firm where I provide professional people of faith the practical leadership development tools and the spiritual fuel they need to amplify their impact in their work environments. Several months later in the fall of 2018, I *finally* joined that international learning and development company and rose quickly into a leadership role. Within a couple months of joining the learning and development company, I was tapped to lead a CEO peer advisory group in New York City for venture-capital backed start-up companies. Fast forward to summer 2019, and through my corporate clients and my weekly podcast, The Graceful Hustle, I was serving hundreds of executives each month, coaching them to become excellent leaders while keeping their souls intact. I was incredibly happy professionally, personally and spiritually. I really believed I'd hang out in this space forever when I got a text that would shift the course of my career once again.

Divine Connections

"I just came across something you'd be perfect for!" It was my business bestie, Kiki Peterson. Kiki and I still haven't quite figured out how we initially became acquainted with each other, but we first officially met when she was interviewing for a spot at the same learning and development company I was working with.

Before this, Kiki and I were connected on Linked In and Facebook friends, but we'd never actually met or even had a conversation. When Kiki, a super talented leadership expert in her own right, began seriously considering joining the learning and development company, its leadership recommended she speak with me as part of her decision-making process. To say we hit it off right away would be an understatement. Kiki and I would not only go on to become professional colleagues, but also spiritual, business and personal sounding boards for each other, laughing with and praying for each other all the way. To say I love her to life would be an understatement.

One day, Kiki was online investigating opportunities to expand her consulting business when she came across an incredible role that would leverage each of my business, executive coaching, and ministry backgrounds. Fast forward to today, and thanks to Kiki and the Lord, I have the joy of leading Christian CEOs and business owners in making better business decisions, creating solid growth plans and thriving in their calling to make an impact beyond their company's bottom line through marketplace ministry. I'm beyond thrilled to be helping Christian CEOs and business owners build excellent businesses for an eternal purpose, and impacting thousands of people in the process.

My work today is exactly what I so deeply desired – it puts me squarely at the intersection of The Greatest Commandment and The Great Commission. It's the fulfillment of the very vision God placed in my heart over a decade ago – to use the leadership skills I was acquiring in Corporate America to build His kingdom.

And while I loved working at my local church and still miss my congregation terribly, I have absolutely no doubt that I'm where I'm supposed to be, doing what I'm called to do in this season of my life. I awaken every single morning with a strong, clear sense that I'm honoring the time God has graciously extended to me on this earth, living out my purpose with vitality and impact. I'm experiencing my John 10:10 preferred life. I'm praying my journey encourages you to pursue your John 10:10 life by maximizing every moment and honoring the time God has graciously given you.

Do Your Work

In what area(s) of your life have you failed to honor the time God has extended to you? Where have you been hiding your talent and playing small because you're afraid? Where have you been criminally cautious? What process will you use – prayer, fasting, wise counsel, due diligence – to discern what God wants from you in this season of life? Turn to Section8 of The Snatch Back Notebook to journal your responses to these important questions.

Once you've reached this critical milestone of committing to maximize every moment, it's essential to Operation Snatch Back that you protect your time. Let's head into our next chapter to learn the mindset shifts and methods that have allowed me to guard the gift of time God has

given me.

Chapter 9

Protect Your Time

We all have that thing. Or maybe it's not a thing. Maybe it's a person, or an obligation. Whatever it is, it drains your energy, sucks up your time and works your nerves. Or maybe it does none of those things, but it just doesn't move, inspire or fill you like it once did. Sure, we all have to do some things we'd rather not. It's part of adulting.

But if you're lacking vitality and failing to have an eternal impact, take a cold, hard look at your life. And I'll bet you any money you're spending way too much time on stuff that's no longer serving you or life purpose well. It could be an organizational commitment that you just can't honor anymore, like being president of your condo association. Perhaps it's a standing social commitment, like a weekly girls meet-up, that you just don't have time for now that you're back in school. Or maybe there's that person in your life that constantly calls with problems but never implements any of the solutions you discuss.

Yes, being involved in our communities, hanging with friends and being there for other people are all good things, but not when we allow them to interfere with and distract us from doing our God-thing. Life is full of opportunities to do good stuff, but our goal with The Snatch Back is to be primarily occupied with "God stuff" – those things that are in line with and fostering the fulfillment of our God-given purpose in pursuit of living our John 10:10 life.

While God is an eternal being that stands outside of time, we're not God. As humans, we're very much bound by time and the constraints it imposes as a precious limited resource. "Time is money" goes the age-old adage. So let's work with that, shall we? Resources like money can either be invested, expended or wasted. I define investment as any use of a resource that yields a profit (e.g., you invest $100 in one share of stock and later sell it for $105. Boom! You just made a $5 profit.) In other words, the benefit is greater than the cost. Resources can also be expended with no up- or downside (e.g., you purchase a share of stock for $100 and later sell it for $100). The benefit merely equals the cost. And then there are wasted resources, where the benefit is less than the cost. Your $100 share of stock loses value and you sell it later for $75, losing $25.

If time is money, we should be thinking about our time critically, analyzing our use of it like we would investing our hard-earned coins. A huge component of reclaiming your time is honestly assessing what activities or obligations are an investment, an expense or a waste. And then lovingly but firmly eliminating any use of time that's a waste and responsibly but strictly limiting anything that's an expense. Remember: "'No' might make them angry, but it will make you free. If no one has ever told you, your freedom is more important than their anger."[67]

Whether you realize it or not, a little life is leaving you every moment. In the time it took you to read that last sentence, your remaining life was reduced by three seconds. Time waits for no one, and it doesn't ask your permission to leave. Time just bounces on you with no heads up. So it's hugely important that you take a hard look at how you're using your time.

Busy or Productive?

Productivity is defined as "the quality, state, or fact of being able to

---

[67] Nayyirah Waheed, *Salt*, p.9.

generate, create, enhance, or bring forth goods and services."[68] Sounds worthwhile, doesn't it? Busyness means "having a great deal to do."[69]

Note that productivity and busyness aren't synonymous. I can be very busy, having a great deal to do, without actually accomplishing anything worthwhile. Productivity honors and protects time – it's an investment. Busyness burns through time with nothing to show for it - it's an expense. In order to determine whether I've been productive or just busy, I have to look critically at my output – what have I accomplished in the time elapsed?

Now I'm sure all the bawses reading this book are now mentally running back the list of their accomplishments in the past six months! But hold up, because we're talking *quality* of accomplishments, not quantity. Just because you've been busy doesn't mean you've been productive. And just because you've been productive doesn't mean you've brought your A-game. My accomplishments don't necessarily mean I've lived on purpose, exuded a contagious vitality and had an eternal impact. Accomplishments

---

[68] www.Dictionary.com
[69] New Oxford American Dictionary

have to be evaluated in light of four things: calling, capabilities, potential and goals. Let's use a different analogy: running. My goal may be to run a half marathon while my current capability may be running two blocks. But, with the proper training and diet, I have the potential to complete a full marathon. In this scenario, running just two blocks means I was busy – I expended energy, yet I didn't live up to my full potential. Finishing a half marathon would be an accomplishment – I would have lived up to my capabilities. But completing that full marathon? That's #goals! Why? Because when I cross the marathon finish line, I would have lived up to my *full potential*. What keeps me from completing that full marathon (other than the fact that I despise running)? The same stuff that will hold you back from reaching your goals if you're not careful. Any number of factors can keep us from maximizing our potential and being uber-productive – unexpected setbacks, unforeseen challenges.

But most of us get our time and all the amazing accomplishments it could bring get snatched away by one sneaky lil culprit – distraction.

Stop Thief!

Distraction is anything that keeps you from giving your full focus to something else. When your focus is broken, attention wanes, discipline lags and accomplishment is compromised. A statement by a nineteenth-century psychologist pretty much sums it: "My experience is what I agree to attend to."[70] In other words, what I decide to pay attention to determines my experiences and the sum total of my experiences become my life. According to a recent Harvard Business Review article, attention management is a key component to stress management (and, by inference, good time management):

"To be consistently productive and manage stress better, we must strengthen our skill in attention management. Attention management is the practice of controlling distractions, being present in the moment, finding flow, and maximizing focus, so that you can unleash your genius. It's about being intentional instead of reactive. *It is the ability to recognize when your attention is being stolen* (or has the potential to be stolen) and to instead keep it focused on the activities *you* choose. Rather than

---

[70] William James, *The Principles of Psychology, Vol.1*, 1950.

allowing distractions to derail you, you choose where you direct your attention at any given moment, based on an understanding of your *priorities and goals*. Better attention management leads to improved productivity, but it's about much more than checking things off a to-do list. *The ultimate result is the ability to create a life of choice*, around things that are important to you. It's more than just exercising focus. It's about taking back control over your time and your priorities."[71]

Sounds like Harvard Business Review is down with The Snatch Back. Just sayin'.

So, how do you do the whole attention management thing? The bottom line is in order to more effectively use our time, we must protect it by intentionally choosing what we pay attention to. That means resolutely determining, what's the highest and best use of our gifts and abilities in our current season of life. And then ruthlessly managing both external as well as internal distractions.

---

[71] Maura Thomas, *To Control Your Life, Control What You Pay Attention To*, Harvard Business Review, March 15, 2018, emphasis mine.

"Highest & Best"

"Would you be interested in . . . .?" *"We need someone* to . . ." "Joe can't

_____, so . . . umm, we were wondering if, you know, uh, *maybe*

you could." Sound familiar?

If you're like most of the people I know, someone is always after your

time and talent. But as pastor, author and leadership expert Carey

Nieuwhof says, "No one will ever ask you to complete your top priorities.

They will only ask you to complete theirs." But can you blame them?

You're sharp as a tack, a savage planner, a beast when it comes to

execution and your word is bond. You. Are. A. Certified. Bawse. But why

then are you so overwhelmed, overcommitted and completely over being

everybody's go-to?

Time is our most precious resource because it's the one thing we

simply can't get more of. But most of us don't need more time - we need

to be better stewards of the time we have. Now before you assume this is

just another "download the latest calendar management app, wake up

earlier and grid harder" speech, hear me out. I believe in all that stuff, but

none of that helps if you're busy with the *wrong* stuff. Remember the busy versus productive discussion we just had? Productivity isn't just measured by the number of projects completed or whether you worked to your full potential.

Productivity is also measured against *purpose*. That's right. You get zero credit for being occupied with the wrong stuff. Chefs don't get credit for producing financial statements. Leave that to the accountants. Chefs get recognized and rewarded for creating scrumptious meals. Why? Because as a chef, creating culinary delights is how that chef makes the highest and best use of his or her time, gifts and abilities. Sure, our chef could play accountant from time to time, but it's highly unlikely they'd be recognized or rewarded to the same degree they would be operating in their God-given purpose. Being overcommitted with the wrong stuff won't just leave you overwhelmed, it leaves you living beneath the full potential and purpose you were designed by God to fulfill. Being overcommitted is a sure-fire way to drain your vitality and blunt your eternal impact. Being busy with the wrong stuff leaves you living somebody else's life, not yours.

Always remember: Everything that's on your plate right now is there because you said "yes" to it at some point. Whether you actually parted your lips, simply nodded your head or merely gave an unintelligible

grunt is beside the point. Point is: you didn't register a loud and clear no.

Saying yes when you should say no makes you miserable and salty. Not

cute, Boo. Ironically, my 2017 medical leave gave me time to think about

how I was stewarding my life and managing my time. As I reviewed the

two years prior, I realized I'd allowed my plate to be piled up with things

that certainly blessed other people, but drained me. Acknowledging that

was a real game-changer for me. Not only did it make me own the fact that

I was complicit in my over-scheduled life, but it also empowered me. The

same mouth I used to say "yes" could be used to lovingly and firmly say

"Thank you, but no." And yet, going around like a defiant toddler saying

no at every turn could cause us to reject some expansive opportunities.

Not a good look either.

So how will you know what to say yes to and what to run away

from like your hair is on fire? How will you consistently identify what

your priorities should be? How can you tell if you're spread too thin? How

can you tell the difference between a good thing to get involved in and a

God thing? Like an overprotective big brother vetting your prospective love interests, you need a process to help qualify the opportunities that come your way, eliminate the undesirables and snatch your time back.

So before you say yes to that next engagement, role, title or other obligation, simply ask a few questions to make sure you protect your precious time and position yourself to make the highest and best use of it:

Question #1: "Does it fit within my *life purpose*?"

Ephesians 2:10 says "God planned for us to do good things and to live as he has always wanted us to live." Remember, your life purpose is the reason you are on this planet. It's the gift you are meant to bring to the world. When you operate in your God-given purpose, you do the things God planned for you to do and live the way God wants you to live, making His plan for this world more complete.

Back in Chapter 2, we talked about finding your signal and I challenged you to develop a life purpose statement. A life purpose statement is an extremely powerful tool, providing you with a path for success and giving you permission to say no to things that are distractions from your divine assignment. Because it defines who you are and what you do, your life purpose statement serves as your true north should you start to stray. So before you accept commitment #154, just slowly tell your multi-talented self: "Self, just because you *can* doesn't mean you *should*." Now, breathe. Pull out your life purpose statement and evaluate this new opportunity in light of your divine assignment. If it doesn't further, enhance or fit in with your life purpose, it's a hard, but loving, "no."

Question #2: Does it honor *my values*?

Your values are not about what you do - values are about who you are. While your life purpose statement will certainly be reflective of some of your values, value clarification is a deeper dive into what's truly meaningful to you and why. Your life purpose I'd about who you are and what you do. Your values lay the parameters and standards within which you will perform your life purpose. When your values are clearly defined and you're committed to living in alignment with them, both macro and micro decision making becomes so much easier. For example, your life purpose may be to develop excellence in processes, teams and individuals. One of your values may be spending more quality time with family. If presented with the opportunity to become the CEO of a company, you'll have to weigh whether that opportunity supports or conflicts with your

THE SNATCH BACK: RECLAIMING YOUR LIFE ONE TRUTH AT A TIME

family time value. When you're asked to do something that doesn't align with your values (no matter how "good" it may be), you can simply say "Thanks, but I'll pass. I'm just not about that [fill in the blank] life." So pull out the values list you created in Chapter 7 and put the opportunity in front of you through the paces.

Question #3: Is it essential to my or my family's *vision and strategic plan*?

Your life vision is the expression of your life purpose and values. Your vision for your life conveys *how* you see that purpose and those values being lived out. But having a vision for your life simply isn't enough, because with a vision without a plan for achieving it is just a hallucination. No mind-altering substances allowed here.

Enter your strategic plan - the step by step guide for how your vision will be realized. Unless you want your vision to turn into a mirage, you need a plan with clear goals, milestones, deliverables and timetables. If someone or something wants your time, run the opportunity through the filter of your vision and strategic plan. If it doesn't match up, bounce it like you would an unemployed, ugly dude with missing teeth tryna ask

you out. NEXT!!!

If you've answered no to any of Questions 1-3, lovingly but gently

break the news that, while you'd love to help, they'll have to find another

victim. If you've answered yes to at least two of Questions 1-3, move on

to Question #4. This opportunity *could* be for you.

Question #4. "Do I *want* to do it?"

Yeah, I realize this is a tricky one. Why? Because some of us, especially

Christ-followers, are so dialed in to living a life of sacrifice that we often

feel guilty thinking about what we want. When faced with an obligation or

request for our time that we have the capacity to fulfill, many of us feel

it's somewhat selfish to inject our happiness or desires into the decision of

whether or not to oblige. Simply put, many of us have never given

ourselves permission to think about what we want, let alone set up

situations to actually *do* what we want. But when we get our life purpose,

vision and plans in line with God's heart, we position ourselves for that

exact set up. Check out Psalms 37:4: "Do what the Lord wants, and he will

give you your heart's desire." God actually honors what we want, because

204

it's in line with what *He* wants. So take a deep breath, smile and ask

yourself, "Is this something I even want to do?"

Question #5. "What would have to be sacrificed in order for me to do this? And am I willing to make those *sacrifice(s)*?"

One of the first rules of snatching back your life is recognizing that

everything has an opportunity cost. Time is a finite resource. Whether we

realize it or not, saying yes to one thing often means saying no to

something else. Taking that extra assignment at work might give you more

money, but it means less time for relationships. What to do? (That values

clarification would be really helpful right about now.) When you're

committed to snatching back your time, you must assess every

commitment in light of its opportunity cost. Luke 14:28 teaches "But don't

begin until you count the cost. For who would begin construction of a

building without first calculating the cost to see if there is enough money

to finish it?"[72] You'll either sacrifice for the life you want or the life you

want becomes the sacrifice. So choose prayerfully and carefully.

---

[72] New Living Translation

Question #6. If I don't do this, *who else can?*

If your answer to either Questions 4 or 5 was "no," then it's time to pass. When presented with a request, many of us (especially women) often battle guilt if we can't fulfill it. This means even if we muster up the courage to decline, we usually go into "fix it" mode, racking our brains for who else could possibly do it. Let's get clear: whose responsibility is it to find someone else if you won't? NOT. YOURS. (That right there should set you free.) However, assessing who else might be positioned for the opportunity will help you do two things: (1) conquer any residual guilt from saying no and (2) realize that there are very capable others who can step in when you can't. Now just put that superhero cape away until further notice.

Forcing myself to answering these six questions about every opportunity that comes my way has done wonders to help me eliminate distractions so I could intently focus on fulfilling my God-given purpose and having an eternal impact. And I'm positive they'll guide you to make the highest and best use of your gifts and abilities, and help you snatch your time back, too. Once you've eliminated the time wasters and limited the time expenses by determining the highest and best use of your time, you need to effectively manage what's left. Protecting your time requires that you put yourself and your God-given purpose on the agenda in a focused and intentional way by eliminating as many distractions as possible.

External Distractions

External culprits like email, social media and text messages will slaughter your productivity before you even realize what hit you. Ever slide onto Facebook for a few minutes to see what your people are up to, only to realize you've been laughing at memes and taking personality quizzes for the past two hours? That scrolling is mad addictive! And if you're managing a dozen different inboxes like me, email can be a total time suck. Jealously guarding your time is one of the best gifts you can give yourself. But it isn't just about you and keeping your calendar uncluttered. Guarding your time will allow you the space and energy to relentlessly focus on fulfilling your God-given purpose. And this relentless focus will bring about faithfulness and excellence that will be a huge blessing to those you've been placed on this earth to serve. Eliminating those external distractions allows you to be of even *greater* value to them. It's about being an excellent steward of the time God has given you.

When it comes to eliminating external distractions, it's so easy in today's hyper-interconnected world to resign ourselves to being perpetually distracted. Yes, the reality of being so connected and accessible 24/7 means there are some encroachments on our time that we can't just get rid of. But the key to eliminating external distractions is to focus on what you *can* control. And on a daily basis, you can control more than you think. Here are seven strategies – I call them my "Seven P's of Productivity" - I've used over the last two years to guard my time and greatly minimize external distractions so I can focus on work that advances my God-given purpose:

The Seven P's of Productivity

(1) <u>Discover your PRIME hours</u>. Every day has twenty-four hours, but not each hour is created equally. Each person has a unique energy flow that sets the rhythm for his or her day. That rhythm will determine whether you're naturally an early riser or a night-owl. That energy flow will determine whether you're naturally most alive before dawn or if you're most energetic when the sun is shining brightest around noon. Somewhere around mid-career many of us discover whether we're early to bed/early to rise types,

or if we really don't get cranking until 11 pm after the household is asleep, or somewhere in between. But if you're not sure which category you fall into, pay close attention to your energy levels throughout the day: When are you able to focus most intently? What time of day do you feel most energized? When do you feel most creative? When are you able to think the clearest? These are what I call your prime hours. These are the times of day that will allow you to do your highest and best work in the most excellent way. These are the hours to be fiercely guarded on your calendar. Section 9 of The Snatch Back Notebook has a space for jotting down your observations around this. After paying attention to my energy flow, I've discovered my prime hours are between 10:0 am and 3:30 pm. Once you've identified your prime hours, you need to figure out what you should be doing during those prime hours.

(2) <u>Identify your PRINCIPAL tasks</u>. Just like all hours in the day aren't created equally, neither are all of your tasks. One key to eliminating external distractions is to clearly identify the relative importance each task holds in the grand scheme of your life and

work. To do this you must evaluate whether the task is crucial to you making the highest and best use of your time. In other words, ask yourself "Does this task further my God-stuff?" "Does it contribute directly to the achievement of my long or short-term goals?" Many people get tripped up and distracted from what's most important because of what's been referred to as "the tyranny of the urgent."[73] Urgent tasks are particularly distracting because by nature they demand immediate attention. Sometimes these tasks contribute to or overlap with your principal tasks, but often they're just other people's priorities, not yours. A tool that many have used for decades to determine the urgent versus the important is The Eisenhower Matrix (Exhibit 1). Named after one of the most famous American presidents, Dwight D. Eisenhower, this matrix helped him sort through his various activities and tasks so he could clearly identify what was most important.

---

[73] Charles E. Hummel, *The Tyranny of the Urgent, Revised and Expanded*, 1994.

Exhibit 1

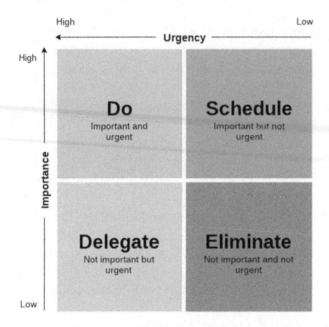

The top half of the quadrant represents those tasks,

obligations or commitments that are most important. These

important items will include some things that are crucial to you

making the highest and best use of your time, like finishing your

business proposal, completing your dissertation or spending

uninterrupted time with your 10-year old. These important items

will also usually include some stuff (okay, lots of stuff) that's very important, but completely unrelated to your life purpose, like

managing your elderly parents' finances or selling your house.

But just because something is very important doesn't mean

it requires your immediate attention today. Therefore, important

items can be further subdivided by the vertical axis into urgent

versus non-urgent important tasks. The key to consistently

eliminating external distractions is to distinguish the important,

urgent tasks (upper left quadrant) from the important, non-urgent

tasks (upper right quadrant). Those important, urgent tasks get

done today, while the important, non-urgent tasks get scheduled on

your calendar for a future time once the urgent, important tasks for

the day are completed.

The bottom half of the matrix relates to unimportant tasks.

How do we deal with non-important stuff? Repeat after me:

delegate or eliminate. Those tasks that aren't important but are

urgent (bottom left quadrant) are a black hole of distraction that

can cause you to blow your whole day. Why? Because the tyranny

of the urgent is screaming in your ear. The way to overcome this

distraction is to delegate the task to someone else - a suitable co-worker, helpful neighbor, willing spouse or responsible child. All that matters is it gets done, but not by *you*. For those tasks that are not important and not urgent? Boy, bye. Eliminate these from your life. Notify whomever you need to, but let it be known - you will not be doing this going forward. Point-blank, period. Use Section 9 of The Snatch Back Notebook to categorize the stuff on your to-do list using the Eisenhower Matrix.

(3) Set your PRIORITIES. Tasks are innumerable. Priorities are few. How do you make a task a priority? You schedule it on your calendar. This means important, urgent, God-stuff tasks become priorities only when we give them a slot on our calendars.

But not just any ole time slot. Those tasks that are most important and urgent, those that are essential to your God-stuff, those that require the most creativity, thought or focus? To get these done right, they require and deserve the best version of you. So map those principal tasks to your prime hours, and do nothing else during this time. That's right, during your prime hours, you work on only those things that move the needle for the highest and

213

best use of your time. Avoid scheduling unrelated meetings, taking phone calls, opening email or other distractions during this time. Again, see Section 9 of The Snatch Back Notebook for a tool to help with this exercise. Now, you won't always be able to execute this flawlessly. Each of us has a different work schedule and responsibilities, leaving some of us with less control over how we structure our day. Hey, if the boss requests something, you gotta respond, right? But to the extent you can, start establishing the habit of blocking your calendar and scheduling your God-stuff during your prime hours. And if you get knocked off track by a competing priority that you just can't avoid, try setting a timer for how long you'll spend on that thing. Then jump right back into your God-stuff. Schedule it like a priority and then treat it like one.

(4) Set up your PLACE. You may hang out in an executive suite or be in a cramped laundry room that doubles as your home office. Regardless of how your situation is set up, make sure it's setting

you up for success, not more distraction. This is less about aesthetics and more about functionality.

Your space needs to be conducive to uninterrupted workflow. This means you should scope your work carefully for the time you've allotted, and only bring what's necessary to complete that work into your workspace. If you can do so efficiently, try to work off-line so you won't get distracted by email or web-browsing on your computer. Turn your phone off or put it on, do not disturb, and leave it in another room. If it's really hard for you to separate from your phone, lock it in a desk drawer and give the key to an assistant or co-worker with strict instructions not to return it to you until you can demonstrate that the allotted work has been completed.

Make sure the room thermostat is set at a comfortable temperature and bring your snacks, water - whatever you need to work in a focused and uninterrupted way. The bottom line is you don't want to have to leave your place during your time and risk getting distracted by a trip to the break room or the fridge.

(5) <u>Make your PLAN</u>. Scope the work you want to complete during those hours – be realistic about what you can accomplish in the allotted time, but don't go too easy on yourself. Make a good stretch goal and compete with yourself to see how much you can actually get done. Decide ahead of time how frequently you'll take short breaks & set a timer for each one so you come back quickly and don't get off course.

(6) <u>Make your PROCLAMATION</u>. Set your intention for your time and let your people know. Put your assistant, your co-workers or your kids (if you're working from home) on notice that they enter your place at their own risk. You can even put a sign on the door. Bottom line: let folks know that you're hunkering down for X period of time and you're not to be interrupted unless the building is on fire or Michelle Obama is calling you to go on tour with her.

(7) <u>Keep your PROMISE</u>. Don't come out of the cave until the defined work block is done. This doesn't mean you have to pull an all-nighter, but it does mean you adopt a mindset that says "you're

finished when it's done." Not leaving until it's done will also help you better scope your future work. If you allot two hours to finish your proposal, but it actually takes you three hours, you'll be able to more accurately scope and schedule your work next time. You owe it to yourself to stop breaking promises to yourself. Keep your word that you'll take this time to focus on your God-stuff without distraction.

Internal Distractions

We all get the concept of external distractions. But what are internal distractions? Whether you realize it or not, that constant barrage of external distractions has conditioned us to *expect* to be distracted by an external stimulus on an average of every forty seconds or so, creating a significantly reduced attention span, even if no such external distraction exists at the moment. As a result, we're always expecting to be distracted, so in short, we've been trained to distract ourselves. That dynamic, coupled with the number of internal thoughts we have every day, leaves us more unfocused than ever. So in addition to doing the things we just learned to limit the external distractions, we desperately need to learn how to limit internal distractions. And in order to do this, we need to master the art of corralling our thoughts.

I never realized how big of a distraction my internal thoughts were until I started working from home exclusively about two years ago. For so long I attributed my lack of focus to outside factors. But working from home with no colleagues dropping by, no assistant poking her head in and no urgent calls from the boss, revealed *I* was the distraction!

Have you ever walked into a room for something only to forget why you came in the first place? Or open your email account only to forget whether you planned to read or send a message? This kind of stuff would happen to me all the time, so for years I thought my short-term memory was shot. But as I began to pay attention to what I was paying attention to, I realized I didn't have a poor memory. The reason I couldn't remember why I'd left my third floor office to go to my first floor library was because, in the minute it took me to walk there, I'd have at least three intervening thoughts! I was constantly allowing my internal thoughts to distract me. My problem wasn't memory-related, it was *focus-related*. I recognized that controlling my internal thoughts was important, not just for my spiritual health as we saw in Chapter 3, but also for my productivity.

One practice that has helped me control my internal thoughts and minimize the distractions that would eat into my time is meditation. I know, I know. Christians reading this book are like, "Nope. I'm not sitting with my legs folded, holding beads and chanting." But that's not what I'm talking about. When I say meditation, I'm talking about the practice of purposefully directing one's thoughts toward a fixed object or focus. And while the word meditation today typically conjures up images of Eastern religions and mysticism, mediation is absolutely a Biblically endorsed practice.

In several passages of scripture we see the admonition to meditate on God's Word, meaning to deliberately direct one's thoughts toward a predetermined point of focus by ruminating, musing or rehearsing that thought. (Refer back to Section 4 of The Snatch Back Notebook for some guidance on how to meditate on God's Word.) So how does meditation help with minimizing internal distractions that can suck precious time away from your God-stuff? The practice of meditation builds your ability to focus, not just on God's Word, but on whatever you decide to apply your focus to. Your ability to focus is like a muscle. I can use my physical muscle to pick up a twenty-five pound dumbbell or I can use it to lift a small child. Same muscle, different object of attention. It's the same with your meditation muscle. You can use it to focus on God's word throughout the day, and you can use it to focus on your God-stuff to minimize internal distractions. Same muscle, different object. The practice of meditation has helped me not only train my brain to lock in on one internal thought to the exclusion of everything else, but also stay locked in on the task at hand until it's done.

But we're human and meditation isn't fool-proof against distractions. So what about the occasional random thought that pops into your head while you're locked and loaded in your designated place, ready to do your God-stuff? Like the random thoughts that pop up, the non-urgent/important things you can't get anybody else in your life to do, like sending in your car insurance payment or making your kids' doctor appointments. This stuff all needs to be done, just not while you're handling your God-stuff business. Inevitably, I'd be cranking out a talk or prepping for a client call when a thought about something I'd forgotten to do, like registering the kids for summer activities, would pop into my head (aka an internal distraction). Old me would stop what I was doing, jump on my iPad and register the kids right then and there, interrupting my flow and taking me twenty minutes to get back on track with my important work. Then I got smarter. Not-so-old me would pull out my iPhone to set a reminder to register the kids for said summer activities, only to be distracted by something else. Bottom line: Not-so-old-me was still falling for the okey-doke. Enter the good ole pad and pen. Now, the current me, keeps a small physical notebook and pen handy to record the interrupting thoughts so I don't lose track of it, but still stay focused on the task at hand. Then, that list of urgent but not-critically important stuff gets scheduled during my non-prime hours.

Time Waits For No One

It's been said that the clock is a soulless mechanism.[74] Time doesn't care who you are, how you feel or what your likes and dislikes are. Time demands that we respect it by waiting for no one. In order to reclaim your purpose, live with vitality and have an indelible impact, you must snatch

---

[74] Tahar Ben Jelloun, The Sand Child, 2000.

back your time clearly identifying what would be the highest and best use of your time, and then fiercely guarding against any external or internal distractions that would take you away from it. Only then can we live our John 10:10 life.

Now in our final section of this book, we'll take a hard look at the third and final area needed for a successful Operation Snatch Back – reclaiming our trust.

PART III

Reclaiming Your Trust

Chapter 10

In God

As much as I love the summer season, there's something about fall. Aside from the fact that my kids are back to school and therefore no longer home all day asking to be fed every hour, I do look forward to fall for other reasons. Not the reality of fall, which in New Jersey signals the cooler temperatures I dislike, but the significance of fall. New season, new classes, new teachers, new school supplies, new school clothes. To me, fall represents a fresh start. It's like getting a chance to hit the reset button without having to wait all the way until January. Every fall, I take the time to reflect on the seasons of life - my journey, where I've been, where I am and where I'm headed. And whenever I do that, this verse always comes to mind: "God makes everything happen at the right time. Yet none of us can ever fully understand all he has done, and he puts questions in our minds about the past and the future." Ecclesiastes 3:11[75]

That verse speaks to me on so many levels, but as it relates to trusting God it really challenges me to trust God's *timing*. Yeah, I struggle to believe that God will do certain things in my life. But even when I know that I know that I know God promised He will do something in my life, I still struggle with "when God, when?" For many of us, our issue with trusting God boils down to simply not trusting His timing. So it's through meditating on this verse that I've begun to look at time in a different way.

I've come to realize that time exists for more than merely providing us with a chronological reference point. In other words, the concept of time doesn't exist just so that we can tell the difference between today and yesterday. What I've begun to realize is that *time is an agent for purpose*. It's God's sovereign hand working through time that brings us to where we need to be in every season of our lives to do the God-stuff He planned for us to do. It's God's providence at work over

---

[75] Contemporary English Version

time that allows us to live out our God-given purpose, have an eternal impact and exude a contagious vitality. And God does all of this in His timing and in His own way. It's how we get to our John 10:10 preferred life.

Spoken In Eternity, Manifested In Time

God is the supreme eternal deity who stands outside of time. He's not bound by it, neither is He limited or enhanced by it. When you are an eternal being you have no need for the concept of time (how cool would that be?). So we can reasonably conclude that God created time as a module in which man would dwell. What our eternal God does is determine in eternity that something will be done, and then He causes that something to manifest in time.

When we read verses like Revelation 13:8 which says that the Lamb (Jesus) was slain before the creation of the world, we understand before the earth was ever formed, before Adam and Eve were ever created, before the sin problem ever got started, God had a plan. Our eternal God, who stands outside of time, had already determined *in eternity* that Jesus would be killed *in time*. And then God set in motion every circumstance, every event necessary for what He already predetermined in eternity would be manifested in time.

His Word Frames My Seasons

We know there is creative force in the spoken Word of God to call into existence that which previously didn't exist. It doesn't get any clearer than Genesis 1:3, "And God said, Let there be light: and there was light."[76] In fact, our God is so creative that we're still discovering planets today that He spoke into existence millennia ago. It's as if God is the orchestrator of an eternal treasure hunt, and every time mankind thinks he's exhausted the depths of God's creation, God says "Let me show you a little bit more!"

But it's not until we better understand scriptures like this next one that we begin to fully appreciate the magnificent power and authority resident in the spoken word of God:

"By faith we understand that the *worlds* were framed by the word of God." Hebrews 11:3[77]

---

[76] King James Version
[77] King James Version, emphasis mine

In Hebrews 11:3 the word "worlds" doesn't just mean the universe. In the Greek, that word "worlds" also refers to "eons" or "ages." In other words, God spoke a word not just to create the physical world in which we live - the planets and galaxies. That's Genesis 1. But Hebrews 11:3 tells us that God has also spoken a word that determines the periods, ages, dispensations, the stages of this world. So the times of this entire universe's existence were all framed by the spoken word of God. That's so deep!

Today we have the Bible, the written word of God, or "logos" word as it's called in the Greek. It gives us our Christian doctrine and instruction for Christian living. But just as important as that logos word and the word that God spoke to frame the periods or stages of this universe, He's also spoken a word that determines the periods or the stages of our lives. Why? Because we serve a God who is interested and active in the affairs of mankind generally and in the lives of His born-again children specifically.

Ever heard somebody talk about receiving a "rhema word" from God and secretly wondered "What the heck is that all about?" but didn't ask? Lemme help you out. In addition to "logos," the Greek word "rhema" is also used for "word" (confused you already, right?). Rhema means utterance. Rhema is an utterance that's not specifically found in Scripture but must *always* be supported by a correct and balanced interpretation of Scripture. Rhema is the word God has spoken to your heart. It's a word that is personal to you.

So God speaks through His written Word, the Bible, which is the most reliable source of God's voice. But God also speaks specifically to our hearts in line with His written Word. Just like God's spoken word in Genesis 1 framed the oceans and just like in God's spoken word framed the ages of this world in Hebrews 11, the rhema you receive from God creates the stages of your life. And that word frames and sets the boundaries for each season in your life.

That's why the Psalmist David was able to declare with confidence, "My times are in Your hands, God.[78]" Your seasons, your future - what you go through, when you go through it, how long you stay in it and when you come out of it – is all framed by the word that God has spoken over your life.

---

[78] Psalm 31:15a, New International Version

It's the word God has spoken over your life that causes all things to work together for your good. The word that God has spoken over your life is why "nothing happens to you, it happens for you." That doesn't mean that everything in your life goes exactly how you want it to. It doesn't mean that bad things haven't happened to you in the past. And it doesn't mean unpleasant things won't happen to you in the future. But it does mean that when you know the word that God has spoken to your heart, it gives you the perspective and the power to reframe the awful, the unfortunate and the unforeseen in light of that rhema word.

And that right there is a game changer. Why? Because it means you get to decide how you're going to react to the bad thing that has happened to you. You get to decide if that bad thing *defines* you or *refines* you. You get to decide if you're going to be a victim or a conqueror. Allowing the unfortunate to refine you into a conqueror means you can trust what God is doing in your life. And most of all, you can trust His timing.

The Proceeding Word Of God

When I was coming up, if somebody was eavesdropping on your conversation with another person and staring at you while you were talking, we'd say to them, "Why you all up in my mouth?" (Warning: there's a minimum melanin level required to pull this off authentically.) If you're going to reclaim your trust in God's word and timing for your life, you need to be all up in God's mouth. Jesus knew a thing or two about this:

"But He answered and said, "It is written, 'Man shall not live by bread alone, but by every word that proceeds from the mouth of God.' "[79]

That means we need to be all up in God's written word so we can accurately discern the rhema word that God has spoken for our purpose and everything else impacted by it, including our families, careers, finances, ministries, health.

Isaiah 55:10-11 says, "As the rain and the snow come down from heaven, and do not return to it without watering the earth and making it bud and flourish, so that it yields seed for the sower and bread for the eater, *so is my word that goes out from my mouth: It will not return to me empty, but will accomplish what I desire and achieve the purpose for which I sent it.* "[80]   When God speaks a word to your heart based on

---

[79] Matthew 4:4, New King James Version
[80] New International Version

what He planned in eternity for your life, that word goes past your mistakes, through your issues, around your insecurities and over your limitations, to manifest in time. That means the word God has spoken over your life doesn't stop because you get sick, become frustrated and tired, lose your job or can't get registered for classes this semester. It doesn't stop because the person you thought was "the one" broke up with you. It doesn't stop because you hit your head on a rock and messed up. The word that God has spoken over your life is an on-going, proceeding word. That word won't stop until it accomplishes the purpose God determined it would when He spoke it in eternity and framed the seasons of your life.

Time is an agent for purpose and it's just a matter of time before you step into your God-given purpose. However, there's one pesky little problem. And this scripture pretty much sums it up:

"For my thoughts are not your thoughts, neither are your ways my ways," declares the Lord. "As the heavens are higher than the earth, so are my ways higher than your ways and my thoughts than your thoughts."[81]

---

[81] Isaiah 55:8-9, New International Version

The problem we have is God doesn't frame the seasons of our lives the way *we think* He should. The good seasons don't start soon enough and the bad ones don't end quick enough for our tastes. And whenever we're left in a protracted season of difficulty, anytime we feel we've been forsaken, our tendency is to wonder if God's proceeding word has somehow been stopped dead in its tracks. We begin to wonder if He's somehow forgotten about us. And even though we know we walk by faith and not by sight, we begin to doubt whether the word we thought we heard was even real because we don't *see* anything happening.

Stay Woke

In Jeremiah 1:11-12[82], the Lord speaks to a young prophet by the name of Jeremiah, asking "What do you *see*, Jeremiah?" "I see the branch of an almond tree," I replied. The Lord said to me, "you have seen correctly, for I am watching to see that my word is fulfilled."

The almond tree was known as the "wakeful" or "watchful" tree because it blossomed earlier than the other trees. It blossomed in late winter, while most trees didn't blossom until early spring. So the almond

---

[82] New Living Translation, emphasis mine.

tree was a symbol of alertness and activity because it blossomed at a time of year when one would least expect it. That word "watching" in Jeremiah 1 means "alert" or sleepless." It also means "on the lookout." In other words, God is saying "Even when it doesn't look like anything is happening, even when you're in the winter of your life, *trust My timing* because I got you. How do you know I got you? 'Cause I'm always looking out and I won't rest until that rhema word I spoke to your heart comes to pass!" So much of trusting God boils down to trusting His timing. I learned this first hand several years ago.

My Testimony

Back in 2007, my legal career was going well, our family was preparing to expand and Lennon and I were getting ready to buy our second home. Everything was up, up and away. But weeks before we were getting ready to close on our new house, I had a dream that I was laid off from my job. Now, my boss at that time loved me and my recent performance review had been great. I had just received a promotion, a huge raise and a bonus. So the dream just didn't make any sense to me.

But it was so vivid and so real, it frightened me. I told Lennon I didn't think we should close on the house, just in case. But we prayed about it, and he felt we should move forward. And we did.

So here I was, this successful corporate executive, with an important title and making a great salary. The saying "Be careful what you're good at - you could end up doing it for years[83]" comes to mind. I was excellent at something I hated. I also began to have a very strong sense that God was speaking a specific word to my heart (yes, also known as a rhema word; very good, class!). I began to have this unshakeable impression God was calling me to ministry. But I also had an even stronger desire to spend more time with our kids. So with a growing family and overwhelming career demands, Lennon and I decided I would eventually transition out after a set number of years. In the meantime, I would fantasize about somehow getting laid off with a great severance package and going on my merry way.

Shortly thereafter my dream, the company I worked for was no longer doing well and employees were being laid off, so I thought for sure

---

[83] Danielle LaPorte, The Fire Starter Sessions: A Soulful + Practical Guide to Creating Success on Your Own Terms, 2014.

that this would be my exit ramp. But when I raised my hand to get released, instead of co-signing on my plan, management made me all kinds of offers to entice me to stay. Talk about a plan backfiring.

I stayed, but every single day I fantasized about quitting sooner than Lennon and I had agreed upon. God knew what I was up to and spoke to me very clearly saying, "Don't you do a thing. Go. Sit. Down." And He reminded me of the dream I had years earlier - the one where the company and I parted ways with me being laid off, not me quitting. This went on for a few years and every time I got ready to walk out the door, I kept remembering my dream from all those years prior. Then one day in 2012, I was offered a new position. Lennon and I prayed about it and agreed I should take it. Things went well for me for the first six months and then all hell broke loose. I found myself working sixteen hour days in an environment more toxic than a superfund site. I was constantly on edge – physically, mentally and emotionally drained.

And I wanted to quit so badly! But in addition to remembering that I like to eat three times a day and live indoors, I stayed because God wouldn't let me forget the dream I had all those years prior. But the hell I was going through on the new job was so stressful that in early December of that year, I decided I'd stay just six more months, just long enough for some of my financial goodies to vest. As miserable as I was, I mentally conditioned myself to suffer for another half a year. Hey, they don't call 'em golden handcuffs for nothing.

Later that same month, my family traveled home to New Orleans to visit my parents for the Christmas holidays. I knew my daddy had been having some health challenges, but during that visit it became evident that he was not doing well at all. His health was really deteriorating and my mama just couldn't seem to manage all the doctors' appointments and umpteen medications he was now on.

As I sat on the plane heading back to Jersey, I knew I needed to go home more often, but wondered where in the world I would find the time because I worked constantly. Four days later, I had what appeared to be a random encounter with a stranger, in the nail salon of all places. I overheard an older woman talking about how free and happy she felt having left a toxic, hostile work environment. I initiated a conversation with her and we talked about her life and where I was in mine. I proceeded to tell her all about my horrible job situation. This stranger responded with words I'll never forget. She looked me in my eyes and said, "Stop worrying about your finances. You, your husband and your kids will be fine! *That job is a career but it's not your calling.* Leave that job and *go pursue your calling.* Don't wait six months to leave. *Get out now!!"*

Her words disturbed me so deeply because I interpreted them as me having to pull the trigger and quit my job. And even though everything in me wanted to do just that, I was still holding on to the dream I'd had so many years earlier. And, oh yeah, there was this other thing going on with me: I was afraid. Scared to leave the so-called security I thought my job and salary represented. But not even one week after the encounter with this woman, my company and I parted ways in a most financially lucrative manner for me, exactly the way it unfolded in the dream I'd had seven years prior. It was just a matter of time! On my last day at the company, I literally danced in the parking lot, because after almost twenty years, I was finally released from a career that I had grown to loathe! And because I was no longer a slave to that wretched job, I had the freedom to go back and forth to New Orleans to see my father, who at this point was extremely ill.

I mentioned earlier that for years as a senior executive in Corporate America I'd felt God wanted me to use what I was learning to build His kingdom. Although I'd interpreted this as a call to the local church and Lennon and I had served in local church leadership for well over a decade, I'd never really considered what that would look like or what kind of a role I'd take on. That was all about to change.

I'd been laid off for about a few weeks when I began to have a strong impression that God not only wanted me to preach occasionally but was also calling me to become a full-time pastor, a role to which I had never, ever aspired. Honestly, it kinda tripped me out a little. One Wednesday night after prayer meeting, I shared what I was sensing with Carmen, one of my day ones, asking her to pray and swearing her to secrecy. Asking for prayer made sense, but the secrecy was borne out of my own insecurities. At the time, our church had only one pastor who was, you guessed it, male. I had so many questions: What would people think about a female pastor? Did my pastor even believe women should be pastors? Even if he did, what about the denomination of which we were a part? Would my family and I have to leave our church so I could pursue my calling? Could I still wear cute clothes and be a pastor? The list went on and on.

Since I had suddenly gone from working seventy hour weeks to being a stay-at-home mom, I had some free time on my hands while the kids were in school. So with my newfound freedom I begin reading voraciously again. Searching on Amazon, I stumbled across a book about discerning the call to the pastoral ministry. Reading that book turned out to be one of the most impactful things I've ever done. It challenged me, yes. But that book also unequivocally confirmed my calling to become a pastor in that season of my life. I never once looked back on my law career.

At the same time I was feeling the call to full-time ministry, our small local church was growing. And unbeknownst to me, God was moving on our lead pastor's heart to consider me and my husband as pastors. We had no clue. We had never once talked about it with him. But God was watching over His word to perform it. He was lining up every situation. We had been lay elders for many years at our previous church but God knows I never would have even considered becoming a full-time pastor if I had still been practicing law. There's no way my schedule would have allowed it. Only God knew that my daddy would become increasingly ill, that he'd eventually be diagnosed with stage four cancer and given weeks to live, and that I would need to be free to go back and forth to New Orleans to see him in the final months of his life. Being laid off gave me the time to be fully present with him without distraction from an all-consuming job. God's providential timing gave me the gift of time with my father. You can't put a price on that.

God is the master planner and supreme strategist. Only God sees the whole chessboard. And He maneuvers situations and aligns people until all the pieces fall right into the places He wants them to be in – all to fulfill His purpose. When I look back, I realize God's rhema word was framing the seasons of my life. I now see that He was watching over His word to perform it in my life. God was looking out! I wanted to get out of my career way back when, but God determined it would happen in His timing, not mine. God said "now" because that was the time to fulfill the purpose He had for me in a totally different calling that was so much more than a career. And although God has since moved me on from a full-time commitment to pastoring, that pastoral calling was exactly what I needed to be doing in that season of my life. And years later, He's still opening other doors for me to use the gift that He's given me to inform and inspire people, leaving me the happiest and most fulfilled I'd been in over twenty years. It was all just a matter of time.

Ecclesiastes 3:11 says "Yet God has made everything beautiful for its own time. He has planted eternity in the human heart, but even so, people cannot see the whole scope of God's work from beginning to end.[84]" I couldn't see the whole scope of what God was doing when I was in job hell. A big part of trusting God is trusting His impeccable timing. His plan for your life is comprehensive. When He puts it all together - when He speaks a proceeding word over your life that frames your seasons of your life; when that word keeps going until it accomplishes its purpose; when God watches over His word to perform it and looks out for you - nothing is missing. You can trust God's timing. I'm so glad I did. Trust Him, and you will be too.

The Way

In addition to trusting God's timing to fulfill your purpose, another critical aspect of trusting God is trusting His leading. Here's another area about which we have all manner of complaints, especially when the course of

---

[84] New Living Translation

life events isn't following the script we've written. While we know God is omniscient and He really does know the beginning from the end, when we hit a bump in the road we just can't help but wonder "God, are you sure about this?"

Even in my most surrendered moments, even when I think I'm hot on the Holy Spirit's trail following Him all the way, I've often fallen victim to a subtle deception. I've been guilty more than a few times of praying "God, tell me which way to go." Sounds like a good thing, right? Until I remember Jesus didn't say he would tell us the way. Jesus said He *is* the way. When someone tells you the way you can get to your destination based on their directions, but you don't have to take them along with you every step of the way. Why? Because they've already told you how to get there. Often when I've prayed "Lord, show me what to do" I was deceiving myself into thinking I was sincerely desiring to be led by Him. But instead of having Him lead me, what I really wanted God to do was hand me a roadmap outlining every step so I could be on my merry way, sans Him. I wanted to be led by God. I just didn't want to have to be dependent on Him every step of the journey. But when someone is your way, you can't reach your destination without them. Jesus doesn't want to merely show us the way. Jesus wants to *be* our way.

But why in the world would we ever want to go it alone? Why wouldn't you want to walk to your destination following someone you're confident knows the way because he created the very roads you're traveling on? I don't know about you, but during difficult times I often find myself doubting Jesus' guidance. I know He's showing me the way and I may feel a sense of His presence walking with me as I journey along, but let me a hit pothole on the road of life and I start to wonder if Jesus is leading me the *best* way. Over twenty years ago, I read *Knowing God's Will* by M. Blaine Smith and his statement often comes to mind: "It is axiomatic that God leads as much by information he withholds from us as by information he gives." Often God's leading is found in details not fully revealed and in situations of which we have no forewarning. God in His infinite wisdom chooses to withhold some information, knowing that its absence will cause us to make moves that would be otherwise deterred by its presence. Simply put, when we know too much we don't always do what God wants us to do. But God, knowing us the way He does and having an eternal plan so much higher than our plans, will allow just that

245

type of life circumstance and somehow work it together for our good and His glory.

And so it is with our purpose. Knowing full well our natural aversion to difficulty, stress and adversity, God most often leads us into our purpose without full disclosure, lest we become overwhelmed and run from our destiny. When tides unexpectedly shift, circumstances go haywire, challenges seem insurmountable and people all of a sudden start acting funny, there's no need to waste your precious energy panicking or getting salty. Use the opportunity to get clarity, which is so much more helpful in the long run than anger, bitterness or mental paralysis. These unexpected events, that hit us out of nowhere like an eighteen-wheeler running a red light, are what I refer to as "signs on the road of life." It's during these seasons of unexpected, unexplainable difficulty that the enemy of our souls gets in our ear prophesying doom. So we have to be relentless in snatching our minds back from the temptation to forge our own way instead of letting Jesus be our way. Just like signs on our streets and highways give us direction, God uses unexpected and unexplainable situations to direct our lives. Dealing with someone who won't relent? You might be looking at a yield sign. Someone walked out of your life?

Instead of running after them, you might need to hit that u-turn. And some situations are clearly dead ends, leaving you with two choices. You can sit parked and complaining, or you can throw your mental and emotional car in reverse and burn rubber out of there. Disappointed? Use the opportunity to become clear and focused about your direction and your next best move. The choice is always ours. I know the "bitter versus better" expression may be hackneyed, but it's so true. The hope that we have in God's promises and the power we have through His Holy Spirit really can enable us to choose better and reject bitter. And it starts with making the decision to trust not only God's timing, but also God's way.

Chapter 11

In Others

"Lord, I don't want to feel this way anymore. I thought that if my pain touched their lives, I'd feel better. I didn't. I thought that by holding it over their heads, I'd feel better. I didn't. I thought that by telling everyone what had been done to me, I'd feel better. I didn't; it only cost me friends and kept the pain alive longer. I thought if only they'd acknowledge how wrong they've been (and how right I've been), I'd feel better. They didn't, so I felt worse. I thought if only I could understand why I picked such people, I'd feel better. So I read books and talked with counselors but that didn't work, because I then discovered other things that I didn't have the emotional energy to deal with. I thought time would make me feel better. It helped, but it didn't heal, because there were still too many things that triggered old memories. I thought that by moving someplace else, I'd feel better. I didn't. I only changed addresses, not what was going on inside of me. Finally, I did two things, and they worked-not overnight, but gradually, patiently, consistently as I kept doing them, they worked. First, I decided

to forgive-and keep on forgiving-until it didn't hurt anymore. Second, I

cried out to God . . . He heard my cry! Suddenly my mind began to clear

and my emotions began to heal. Why? Because at last I reached the place

where getting well meant more . . . so much more to me . . . than staying

sick!"[85]

Those words spoke to my soul the first time I read them years ago.

In fact, they still grip me to this day. If you've ever been hurt by someone,

I'll bet you can identify with this poignant description of what it feels like

to wrestle with the monster of unforgiveness.

Trust is essential to live out your God-given purpose, have an

eternal impact and exude a contagious vitality because God has called us

to do this in community with others. But it's difficult to fully participate in

the community when we have trust issues. Operation Snatch Back is about

facing the hard stuff head on so you can get to a life of purpose, vitality

and impact. And reclaiming our ability to trust others is so essential to

this. Often our trust issues are because of past hurts. And we regain our

---

[85] Bob Gass, The Word for You Today, 2014.

ability to trust by forgiving. And we forgive others by making a decision to do so, and to keep doing so until it doesn't hurt anymore.

I don't know the nuances of your particular circumstances as it relates to trusting others. But what I do know for sure is this: it's impossible to snatch back our hearts from the hurt inflicted by others and experience healthy trust without forgiveness. For those who violated your trust, forgiveness is required. Christians understand that Scripture teaches we must forgive those who have wronged us if we want God to forgive us of our wrongdoing.[86] But even if you can't get with that, consider this: unforgiveness is a prison we build for others only to find ourselves captive. Bottom line: if you want to live a free, purposed-filled, impactful life, you gotta forgive 'em. But before we take a look at what forgiveness entails, let's take a good hard look at what unforgiveness looks like. But brace up, 'cause it ain't cute.

The Ugly Truth

Unforgiveness rehearses the wrong, whether real or perceived. Unforgiveness keeps going over it, talking about it, replaying mentally

---

[86] Matthew 6:14-15

what was said or done. Maybe you've been there: stewing in it and getting more and more hurt, angry or depressed every time you think about it.

Whenever you get hit in a spot that's already been injured, it hurts even more than usual. The pain can be so intense that it causes you to overreact. When we carry around unforgiveness, we tend to overreact to disagreement, constructive criticism, or any perceived wrong or slight. When we're mired in unforgiveness, just the fear that someone might offend, hurt or disappoint us again causes us to over react. So instead of taking the time to ask her what she really meant or ask him why he did what he did, we operate from our brokenness and presume. In our minds, we don't have to ask her what she meant. We know what she meant based on what we think the last person who behaved that way meant. We don't have to ask him why he did what he did. We presume to know why he did what he did based on why we think the last guy did what he did. And we over-react.

Still others of us use defense mechanisms such as sarcasm, avoidance and shame to mask our unforgiveness. Out of these, avoidance is a biggie. In talking to people over the years, I've seen it used time and time again. Our fear of being hurt or disappointed again causes us to put up walls. Instead of having an honest conversation with the person who hurt us about what happened, we avoid any meaningful interaction with them. When we use avoidance as a passive-aggressive means of punishing the person who hurt us, we withdraw our time, attention and/or affection. Trust me, I'm not saying that each and every slight in life requires a heart to heart conversation, but deep down you and I know which ones merit some resolution. If we're going to ever live free from the toxins of unforgiveness, we must have those tough conversations.

Sometimes unforgiveness looks for sympathy. There's a certain addiction to the attention received from being perceived as the victim. Perhaps you have been legitimately wronged. But having been wronged and adopting a victim mentality are mutually exclusive – they don't have to go hand in hand!

Often unforgiveness looks like a plain ole grudge. Grudges don't have to be some angry, blatant show of emotion. In fact, most grudges are silent and festering. Sure, many of us are sophisticated enough to dress it up, but when we strip down to our bare emotions, we're holding a good ole fashioned grudge.

When we fail to forgive and keep forgiving, our souls die a slow death and we end up carrying around the invisible corpses of dead thoughts, dead habits and dead emotions related to the people who hurt us or the situations that disappointed us. Those dead thoughts, habits and emotions come with narratives that sound like these:

- "Nobody really likes me. I'm just not good enough."
- "I don't know why everybody thinks he's so great. If they only knew what I knew about him . . ."
- "This relationship won't last because everyone eventually leaves me."
- "Did you see/hear what they did to/said about me?"

Do Your Work

What dead thoughts are lurking around in the recesses of your mind? What dead habits are you dragging around, seemingly unable to break free from? What dead feelings are you carrying around in your emotions? Turn to Section 11 of The Snatch Back Notebook and journal your thoughts in response to these questions.

Feel, Deal And Heal

Maybe you've been there. Hurt, disappointed, disillusioned and generally ticked the heck off. And your ability to trust others has been severely damaged. We now clearly know what unforgiveness looks like. But for those of us who decide it's better to reclaim our ability to trust than stay broken, let's examine *forgiveness*.

One of the best definitions of forgiveness I've found is "the *intentional* and *voluntary* process by which a victim undergoes a change in feelings and attitude regarding an offense, lets go of negative emotions such as vengefulness, with an increased ability to wish the offender well."[87]

Many people struggle with forgiving someone because they mistakenly think that forgiveness means they have to condone or excuse the wrong that was done to them. But nothing could be farther from the truth. And while we're at it, let's be clear that forgiveness doesn't mandate

[87] Cynthia Garrett, I Choose Victory: Moving from Victim to Victor, 2020, emphasis mine.

reconciliation or restoration of the relationship involved. Reconciliation requires trust. And while forgiveness is required and reconciliation may be desired, trust must be earned.

In vehicle safety tests, researchers place a crash-test dummy inside a vehicle. Then the vehicle is intentionally crashed into some type of obstacle to see how well both the vehicle and the crash-test dummy fare during the accident. And the researchers don't perform this test just once. They crash numerous of the same vehicle type over and over. And the poor crash-test dummy is always along for the ride. Never forget this: You are not a crash test dummy. When you repeatedly trust people who haven't demonstrated themselves to be trustworthy, it's like those vehicle safety tests we've all watched with you starting as the crash-test dummy. Stop being a crash test dummy for people who keep making a wreck out of your relationship with them. Forgiveness is required for your emotional healing and wholeness, but before you put yourself in a position to be vulnerable with or to them, require that they earn your trust.

However, failure to forgive one person can lead to on-going distrust of innocent others. Unforgiveness is like leaking sewage. It doesn't stay contained to the original relationship or situation that hurt you. Unforgiveness somehow always manages to seep out and stink up everything in a person's life. The telltale signs of unresolved hurt can be seen in a trail of broken relationships, fractured friendships and wounded colleagues, all because of holding unforgiveness towards a person or regarding an incident. When we allow the sewage of what happened to us in one marriage, job or friendship to spill over into our next, we're left with serious relationship and community deficits.

Remember way back when in this book I talked about the soul and how it's made up of our minds, wills and emotions? Well, forgiveness is an act of my will. Once I exercise my will and begin to forgive, that action then causes a change in my feelings & attitude. In order to forgive we have to feel, deal and heal.

Feel

When we feel, we face the wrong that was done to us and we acknowledge the hurt we've experienced. Acknowledging that someone hurt you doesn't make you weak. It makes you human. Failing to be honest and admitting we've been hurt keeps us trapped in a cycle of dysfunction and unresolved issues. So we just push it down and keep going, telling ourselves "I don't

THE SNATCH BACK: RECLAIMING YOUR LIFE ONE TRUTH AT A TIME

really care." "It's not like we were that close anyway." "I'm not beat for a friend - I got plenty."

But I can run on a fractured leg only but for so long until that jagged, broken bone starts pushing through my flesh and pokes out through my skin. And my denying the fracture won't make it any less repulsive or painful. Failing to acknowledge a hurt is like running on a broken leg. Sooner or later, my brokenness pokes out, showing itself in a host of ugly ways. Christians often struggle with acknowledging emotions that we think aren't very "spiritual" (whatever that means). You might be surprised to learn that the Bible allows for anger as a legitimate emotion: "In your anger do not sin."[88] God doesn't expect us to suppress our emotions, but to use self-control in the expression of our emotions. You have to acknowledge that you're hurt in order for forgiveness to even begin to take place.

In order to start the process of forgiveness, you don't need the person who hurt you to admit that they were wrong or even apologize for what they did. Admission and apology are necessary for restoration of a

---

[88] Ephesians 4:26

relationship, but they aren't prerequisites for forgiveness. This is why we can be set free from unforgiveness against someone with whom we have no contact. You can forgive a dead person because there's nothing you need from them in order to forgive. The decision to forgive is all on you. To start the process, you must simply allow yourself to feel. Then it's time to deal.

Deal

In dealing with unforgiveness, understanding the difference between a reason and an excuse is key. A reason explains why something happened. An excuse justifies what happened, and makes it okay. The person who wounded you may have a reason why they did what they did, but it doesn't excuse the wrong. Maybe your parent or guardian was violated as a child and their hurt, pain, fear from that incident so paralyzed them emotionally that they weren't able to nurture and protect you. Maybe they turned a blind eye to some of the things being inflicted on you growing up. That doesn't excuse what they allowed to happen to you. But it is a reason. And sometimes, when our minds are trying to make sense of what's happened, understanding why someone did what they did or why they failed to act helps us to develop compassion for that person. And some amount of compassion is vital for forgiveness.

Dealing with the wrong will also require that we psychologically and emotionally isolate the wrong. Ever stumble around your house in the middle of the night and stub your toe? The sharpness of that unexpected pain can make you want to cut off your whole foot! But that'd be pretty dumb because only a toe has been injured and, unless you ran into the wrong end of a meat cleaver, it can very likely be healed. Some situations really do require that we exit stage left and cut ties altogether, but before you holler deuces, let's work through that a little bit.

Isolating the wrong requires that we judiciously evaluate what needs to be done differently. All men are not bad, not all bosses are narcissistic and not all family members are toxic. Just the ones you've dated, worked for and well, you didn't pick your family members so I really don't know what to say here. But you get the idea. So maybe you need to ask yourself why you keep making the same bad choices and pray for discernment before accepting that next job, date or family dinner invite. Isolate the issue and make the necessary adjustments so you don't make the same less than ideal choices again. When we fail to isolate the wrong, we toss out whole categories of people or opportunities and lose some valuable life experiences in the process. Instead of throwing the baby out with the bath water, isolate.

Heal

Harnessing the amazing freedom that comes with forgiveness is life-changing. But along with that freedom comes the power to choose - the power to choose the type of relationship we want to have, if any, with the person who wronged us. Just because I forgive someone doesn't mean that I have to automatically trust them or even rebuild the same type of relationship we had before the incident, especially if they haven't done what's necessary to regain my trust. Healing requires that we restore the relationship to the extent appropriate, if at all. So while reconciliation is a laudable goal, we must evaluate what degree of restoration is appropriate given the circumstances.

Lastly, to effectively heal we must decide achieving wholeness is more important than staying broken. There's a New Testament account of a man who had been an invalid for thirty-eight years. The Scripture says

"When Jesus saw him stretched out by the pool and knew how long he had been there, he said, 'Do you want to get well?'"[89] Seems like a crazy question, right? I mean, Jesus the man has been sick for thirty-eight years! Why in the world *wouldn't* he want to get well? Jesus knew something we need to learn: Just because someone's sick doesn't mean they want to get well. We'll never pursue wholeness until the discomfort of our current state exceeds our fears of the process to change.

I often tell people that forgiveness is like an onion: it's layered and you'll probably cry a little with each one you peel back. Don't agree? Ever think that you've really forgiven someone only to find that an ugly reminder of your history with that person pops up like Freddie Krueger in a Nightmare on Elm street sequel? Yeah, you thought that thing was dead and buried, but here it is emotionally and mentally terrorizing you again. I'm telling y'all: there's layers to this. Layers to our hurt, layers to our pain, layers to our disappointment. And each layer has to be acknowledged and dealt with. And that's where it becomes vital to make

---

[89] John 5:5, The Message Bible

the same decision Bob Gas made: "to forgive-and keep on forgiving" until it doesn't hurt anymore. We must be relentlessly committed to our healing.

Forgiving And Forgetting

There's an Old Testament scripture which says, *"Forget about what's happened; don't keep going over old history*. Be alert, be present. I'm about to do something brand-new. It's bursting out! Don't you see it? There it is!"[90] I love this verse because it's a great reminder that no matter what's happened, God is always up to something new and wonderful in our lives. The reason your vehicle's windshield is way bigger than your rearview mirror is because what's ahead of you is so much more important than past hurts and regrets will ever be. Learn from them, sure. But once you've got the lesson, *don't keep going over old history!* Developing the habit of forgetting can make the healing process so much easier.

The longer we take to forgive the longer our dysfunction is normalized. Next thing we know, we can't remember a time when we didn't feel this way – angry, bitter, preoccupied, distracted, hurt, rejected, depressed. So whenever someone says, "I can forgive, but I'll never

---

[90] New Living Translation

forget," I'm always more than a tad skeptical. Why? Because I know whenever I've said that, I'm usually still harboring unforgiveness but trying to put on my magnanimous game face. And while we don't need a study of human behavior to tell us forgiving and forgetting go hand in hand, good thing there is one. A study reviewed by *Psychology Today* concludes " . . . forgiveness may actually give people *permission to forget* (emphasis mine)—that is, when people are willing to forgive, they are willing to give up the details of an episode. But when they are *unwilling* to forgive, they keep those details around. Presumably, they will also re-experience those details negatively when they remember them in the future."[91] So when we sincerely forgive someone, it helps us to forget the details of what was done to us. Over time, this forgetting makes it more difficult for the transgression (whether real or perceived) to trigger the energy required to really feel angry at the other person.[92]

While anger may make us feel better momentarily, clarity enables us to do better permanently. It's been said that angry is just sad's

---

[91] Art Markman, Ph.D, *Are We Truly Able to Forgive and Forget?*, Psychology Today, August 5, 2014.

[92] Id.

bodyguard. So exactly what is our anger protecting or hiding? "[A]nger is almost never a primary emotion in that even when anger seems like an instantaneous, knee-jerk reaction to provocation, there's always some other feeling that gave rise to it. And this particular feeling is precisely what the anger has contrived to camouflage or control."[93] Sadness, disappointments and hurts make us all feel assailable and exposed. Rather than deal with the vulnerability of those emotions, we summon anger to defend us against leaning into these uncomfortable feelings. But dealing with those disquieting emotions can ultimately be so freeing. When I face my sadness head on and dig deep to understand the why behind the feeling, it brings me one step closer to clarity. Once I understand why I feel the way I feel, I can begin to take steps toward freedom from those negative, controlling feelings.

God is calling us to live a preferred John 10:10 life, full of purpose, vitality and impact. This requires that we snatch back our trust so we can have healthy, vibrant relationships with those God has called us to serve.

---

[93] Leon F. Seltzer, Ph.D., *What Your Anger May Be Hiding*, Psychology Today, July 11, 2008.

Chapter 12

In Yourself

It was 1993. I was 24 years old and had already had at least one decade under my belt of living a diminished life. Two more years couldn't hurt, I thought. Like most of my fellow law school colleagues, I had spent summers working at major law firms so by graduation I knew full well what to expect – incredibly long hours of first year associate grunt work, all at a salary, which after taxes, allowed me to do little more than pay my exorbitant NYC rent and crushing student loan payments. But unlike most of them, I didn't enjoy the law. I don't mean I didn't enjoy the rigors of law school (only a very strange few do). I mean I didn't like learning about the law. If that wasn't a hint and a half, I don't know what was. Apparently, Monique Carkum Edwards, Esq. didn't take it. Coming to grips with this post-graduation was distressing to say the least, given I graduated with over $110,000 of student loan debt.

How do we start down the slippery slope of living a life we really don't want and learning to accept it as our reality? By failing to trust ourselves. I know I lost some of y'all right there. "Trust myself?"

"Doesn't the Bible say not to put any 'confidence in the flesh'?" Before

you go all "See, I knew she was a heretic" on me, just hear me out.

As believers, God's Holy Spirit supernaturally came to live in our

hearts when we accepted Jesus as the atoning sacrifice for our sinful

nature. Trusting yourself is about trusting that the Holy Spirit inside of

you is speaking and that you hear Him clearly. Trusting yourself is about

honoring that nagging feeling or that thought that you can't get out of your

head no matter how much you pray. Notice, I said honor, not slavishly

obey. Honoring something means you pay it the amount of attention it

deserves. You'd never break your leg and say "I'm good. I'm just going to

ignore the pain. No need to go to the hospital." Never. You wouldn't hack

your broken leg off with a chainsaw (overreacting) but you wouldn't try to

run a marathon the next day pretending you were okay either

(minimizing). The pain in your leg tells you that something is wrong.

You'd honor that pain by going to see an orthopedist and getting the

proper treatment.

So why do we have so much trouble paying attention to our

feelings and giving them the attention they deserve? Breaking news:

You're not a spiritual superhero leaping over difficult emotions in a single bound. Of course, we shouldn't act on every feeling we have or let our feelings wholesale dictate our decisions. If you slapped your annoying coworkers every time you felt the urge, you might have an arrest record longer than I-95. Definitely not a feeling to act on. But you probably should take some time to examine why, per adventure, would you ever want to do such a thing. Maybe you do have deeply rooted anger management issues. Or maybe your gig just isn't right for you and you really need to move on. (All corporate security personnel in favor, say "I.") Wherever the case, we should trust the Holy Spirit inside of us enough to say, "Wait a minute. Let me honor my feelings by taking the time to examine *why* I feel the way I do." When we push down and deny persistent, pervasive feelings we dishonor them, and therefore ourselves. Kinda hard to live free if that's how your situation is set up. Just sayin'.

Part of living our John 10:10 life of purpose, vitality and impact requires that we trust ourselves. Rather than ignore those feelings that signal something just ain't right, we'd better serve ourselves by leaning into them a little. Notice I said lean into, not fall over and drown in them. Pay attention and ask what might those feelings be signaling to you. If every time you walk into a social gathering of certain friends you feel tension, pay attention to that. It doesn't mean they're terrible people, but maybe that's not your hang for right now. If your stomach starts trying out for the USA Gymnastics team every time you attend your weekly staff meeting, it's probably a clue that you're in the wrong role, team or company. Or all three.

Ignore At Your Own Peril

For almost twenty years, I was very successful in a profession I could barely stand – practicing law. Being good at something doesn't obligate you to do it. And certainly not for twenty years. The fact that I would sit in meetings struggling to resist the urge to tell off brown-nosing coworkers and arrogant bosses told me two things: one, I really needed Jesus and two, I needed a new career. But I didn't trust myself. Didn't trust the voice inside that told me I had a gift that would never be appropriately valued in my current place. Didn't trust the gnawing feeling I had that I was created for more. So for years I made a great career and a lot of money, but in the process I dishonored my calling.

Although I did eventually leave the practice of law, several years later after moving into ministry I found myself not trusting myself yet again. When I began pastoring full-time, I thought I'd died and gone to heaven. Not only did I love the work, but I adored the people and I excelled at a number of the job requirements like preaching, counseling, starting and growing ministries and leadership development. If career satisfaction is a combination of doing the right thing with the right people in the right organization, I'd finally hit the jackpot!

But after a few years in the role, I realized that, for a number or reasons, it was time to move on. At the top of that list was my family. As the mother of young children and wife to a husband with a fast-growing law firm, the demands of ministry were completely misaligned with my family's needs. For almost two years, I knew deep down that I needed to make a change, but I didn't trust myself.

For starters, despite all my theological self-studies, I realize I had such an underdeveloped understanding of calling and purpose. Yes, I understood that my purpose was to be spiritual C4, blowing the roof off of possibilities for myself and others. And yes, I knew in my head that I could fulfill that role outside of the church, but deep down in my heart I still internalized local church ministry as the highest and best expression of my calling. Therefore, I felt a self-imposed guilt for wanting to leave it.

That, coupled with the sense of duty and obligation I talked about earlier, kept me in place way longer than I should have remained.

I also have to admit another reason I stayed was because I didn't trust that, despite being resourceful, hard-working, intelligent, relevant and fairly likable (especially on days when I refrain from telling off anybody), I could reinvent myself and pursue my calling outside the four walls of the church. I didn't trust that the longing inside of me to learn, grow and have a different kind of impact was God-ordained, and therefore deserved to be honored, acted upon and cultivated. I kept thinking, "What if this is my flesh talking?" when instead I should have been attentively listening to what my longing was telling me.

But when you doubt yourself, it's so easy to let other things take precedence over what you know you ought to be doing. In fact, your self-doubt will almost compel you to prioritize someone else's demands over your desires. Because after all, that feels safe. Not only does it feel safe, but for Christians it sounds downright noble. I mean after all, doesn't Jesus talk about all that "laying down your life and picking up your cross" stuff?[94] It's amazing how we can spiritualize anything, especially the fear of boldly stepping out on faith into something "non-traditional."

I've learned that trusting myself really boils down to trusting the Holy Spirit inside of me. It's believing that as I develop in my relationship with God by spending time in prayer and His Word, I'm developing the discernment I need to accurately interpret what I'm feeling and make the necessary decisions. It was this process of intentionally seeking God through prayer and reading the Bible that I began to get the confidence and clarity I needed to trust that what I was thinking, feeling and longing for was truly God-ordained and Spirit-led, not flesh-driven.

---

[94] See Matthew 16:24-26

Conclusion

Living The Snatched Back Life

Recently while attending a workshop for leaders, I was asked to describe my life in one word. I hate these types of exercises because in case you haven't noticed, I'm not a "one word" kinda woman. Besides the fact that I naturally think in threes, it's so hard to settle on just one word that encapsulates my feelings about my entire life. But I eventually settled on the word "becoming."

When used as an adjective, becoming denotes beauty and attractiveness, and when used as a verb, the word becoming means to be in the process or state of change. And while my life has certainly been one of evolution, it's been so much more than that. Aristotelianism, the philosophical school of thought named after the famed Greek philosopher Aristotle, articulates "becoming" as change involving realization of potentialities, as a movement from the lower level of potentiality to the higher level of actuality.

This concept of potentiality refers to any possibility that a thing can be said to have. Aristotelianism does not consider all possibilities the same, and places greater importance on those possibilities that have the potential of "becoming" real of their own accord under the right conditions and free from hindering interference.

In executing my own Operation Snatch Back, I learned to acknowledge my potential of becoming. By snatching my thoughts back from self-doubt, fear and other people's opinions, I was able to free my mind from the mental strongholds that hindered me. It was through reclaiming my trust in God's timing as well as learning to trust myself that I was able to break away from the reluctance that hindered me. And by maximizing, honoring, and protecting my time, the right conditions were created for the most important possibilities in my life to be realized.

The Snatch Back isn't about living a perfect life. It's not about mimicking someone else's social media filtered existence, or vainly attempting to create your own flawless, trouble-free existence. Living The Snatched Back Life is about being perfectly fulfilled in the one precious life you've been graciously given by God. And that fulfillment happens in the process of becoming.

Becoming isn't a one and done kind of thing, but instead a life-long process that prioritizes the committed pursuit of the John 10:10 rich and satisfying life Jesus promised us. When you live The Snatched Back Life, you intentionally look for God-directed and approved possibilities, and then you nurture them to fruition by setting up favorable mindset conditions and removing interference in our environments so those possibilities can become realities.

This process of becoming isn't linear or predictable. I often made changes and seized opportunities not knowing exactly where they would take me but trusting that if I made the commitment to live out my purpose on purpose, God would guide me to where I could exude a contagious vitality and have the greatest impact. With each change I learned a little more about myself, but more importantly I learned a ton about God.

I learned that God's plans for our lives are more generous and expansive than we could imagine. I learned that God can redeem all kinds of situations for His glory. And I also learned that there isn't a pinnacle to my purpose. Although God will certainly use the gifts and abilities I've acquired over time wherever He takes me, God will continuously take me back to the bottom rung to start the growth process all over again. It's my never ending journey of becoming.

I hope this book has encouraged you to execute your own process of becoming, learning to place greater importance on those possibilities that have the potential of "becoming" real under the right conditions and free from hindering interference. Remember, continuously we are either, on the one hand, moving forward in our purpose, or on the other hand being existentially kidnapped by the enemy of our souls. Never forget: there is no third hand. Although Operation Snatch Back may be challenging at times, my prayer for you is that your desire to embrace the preferred John 10:10 life would propel you forward into unapologetically bold action. Your preferred life is there for the living. Snatch it back!

Acknowledgements

It's been almost four years since I first started writing a book. I'd start, then get distracted or feel as if I didn't have enough meaningful things to say. Then I'd be momentarily inspired and wistfully think about being an author once again. But my writing never really gained traction. I told myself it was because I loved to speak way more than I loved to write. But the truth was, I had more growing to do.

Over fifteen years ago I was driving to work one morning, when I felt God speaking to my heart. I felt God say, "I'm going to take you in a way you didn't think you would go, in order to teach you some things you thought you already knew."

So when I started writing in 2016, little did I know I *still* needed to allow God to teach me some things I thought I knew. And while I'm sure there are many more lessons to come, I believe in my heart *now* is the time to share what He's taught me so far. Thank you for giving me the privilege of sharing them with you.

There are a few people without whom this wouldn't be possible. In a very literal sense, none of this would have ever happened without my daddy and mama, Curtis and Bernice Carkum. They not only gave birth to me, but those two raised me, trained me and prepared me more than they could have ever realized. My only regret is that I didn't write this book before my daddy passed away. He always told me like his mother, my Grandma Velma, told him, "Don't say you failed, say you tried." Daddy, I not only tried. I succeeded. Happy reading, Mama!

Next up is my husband, Lennon C. Edwards, Esq. Lennon, for twenty-three years, you have consistently been peace, security, protection, stability, support, love, joy, happiness, and laughter for me. You believed when I doubted, encouraged me when I lost hope and comforted me when I cried. Thank you for walking with me and speaking faith over me every step of the way on this journey. I love you more than life itself.

To my children, Brooklynn and Judah. You two are my heart walking around outside my body. I never want to disappoint or set a less than admirable example for you. A huge part of my quest to make the highest and best use of the gifts God has given me is so that you can see it's never too late to grow, develop and move ever forward.

To my sister and brother-in-law, Shelly and Stephen Lombard. Shelly, after mama and daddy, no one has done more to develop me into the person I am today than you. You continue to support me and have never let me settle for less than what God has for me. Your words were life to me when dead issues, dead mindsets and dead attitudes were surrounding me. Stephen, there are people that God has specifically assigned to speak life over me. You are definitely one of them. From our deep conversations about God's Word to your funny and encouraging texts, thanks for being more than a brother-in-law. Thanks for being a friend.

To my spiritual sisters: Carmen Jordan, Sylvia Santana, Debveda Berry-Moore and Maryline Locke. You ladies have always envisioned bigger and greater for me. You've covered me in prayer, spoken forth God's plan for my life and never allowed me to get comfortable. You've celebrated my every victory. Most importantly, you bugged me about getting this book finished. You are my sisters from other misters. I'm forever grateful for your friendship.

And to my editor/writing coach, James Smith, who came along at a critical juncture and was invaluable in pushing this project to the finish line. Thank you, thank you, thank you!

Whenever I felt self-doubt, exhausted or overwhelmed during this process, what kept me going was the thought, "If this book can help just one person reclaim their life, it'll have all been worth it." Thank you, dear reader, for being my inspiration. I hope you have found something helpful amongst these pages. And I hope you'll tell me about it one day.

About the Author

Monique, a recovering corporate attorney and full-time pastor, is the founder of Gravitas Executive Consulting, helping professionals of faith amplify their impact through leadership development, communication strategy and spiritual renewal. Described by her clients as dynamic, impactful and results-focused, Monique has coached countless executives at Facebook, NBC Universal, Microsoft, Delta Airlines, Morgan Stanley, New York Life, American Express, The New York Times, MTV, Sotheby's and many other companies. In addition to Gravitas, Monique serves as a chairperson with an international peer advisory group for Christian business owners and CEOs. A highly sought-after speaker, *The Snatch Back* is Monique's first published written work. She can be heard weekly equipping and inspiring hundreds of professionals of faith through her podcast, *The Graceful Hustle*. When she's not unleashing the greatness in others, Monique loves reading, fashion, laughing out loud with girlfriends, and spending time with her husband Lennon and their children Brooklynn and Judah. Monique and her family reside in South Orange, New Jersey.

To learn more about Monique, visit moniquecarkumedwards.com.

Made in the USA
Las Vegas, NV
04 August 2021

27545800R00166